3/2   100
2

Intransigent and Militant

6o years as a trade unionist

Jack Fawbert

Dedications

This book is dedicated to my very special Dad who is no longer with us, as well as to all those salt-of-the-earth brothers, sisters and comrades who I have worked with, stood on picket lines with, celebrated with and commiserated with in my life as a trade unionist. You have all enriched my life and demonstrated to me what socialism in action really looks like. Solidarity forever!

`Rise like Lions after slumber
In unvanquishable number--
Shake your chains to earth like dew
Which in sleep had fallen on you--
Ye are many -- they are few.'

Shelley (1819)

Contents

Chapter 1

A chip off the old block?

This is the story of my life as an active trade unionist. This year, 2024, I will be 76 years old and, although I have had various occupations during my lifetime and therefore have been a member of several different trade unions, I will have 60 years of continuous, unbroken trade union membership. As with many life-long trade unionists, my background growing up in an overwhelmingly working-class community in a socialist household committed to trade unionism was a very important factor in helping to shape my beliefs and actions.

This is my second autobiographical book, the first being the story of my childhood and teenage years called *Growing up in Dagenham: Recollections of a Baby-Boomer* (Fawbert, 2022). Whilst there will be a small amount of overlap with that book, this account is about something completely different; my adult life, and more specifically my adult life as a trade unionist. It largely takes a chronological approach, although some aspects of my life as a trade unionist do overlap and therefore deviate from the arrangement of events or dates in the order that they happened. So, it may appear to be a bit random from time to time.

I wanted this account to be largely based on my own recollection of events, but after all these years it has got a bit mixed up in my head what are really recollections and what are stories that other people have told me as well as documentary evidence that I have kept over the years. Also, media reports about some events may have coloured my own recollections of my involvement in certain events; especially as the mainstream media tend to distort and denigrate anything that trade unionists do.

So, if I have misremembered anything and it offends anyone, I apologise in advance. Anyway, I've done the best I can to disentangle these various narratives and on occasion had no alternative but to rely on what I have read or been told by others. This is a story of real-life events. So, although I use the full names of some of the people connected to my story, most of the time, sometimes for obvious reasons and sometimes simply because I've forgotten their surnames, I have just used first names.

As I said at the beginning, my socialist and trade union commitments were greatly influenced by my parents' commitment to such values. Although Dad was a Geordie and Mum was from Oldham, they had lived on the giant Becontree council estate in Dagenham (more about that in a moment) since its construction was completed in the 1930s. Like many working-class couples in the inter-war period, my parents had met at the local Wesleyan Methodist Chapel in Dagenham. They were both socialists and, after a period of time in the Independent Labour Party, with which they became disillusioned, they both joined the Communist Party of Great Britain (CPGB) which they remained in for the rest of their lives.

Mum was an expert seamstress, originally a glove maker, and she expressed her socialist views through support for the Cooperative movement, being involved, for example, in organising an annual 'Coop Bazaar'. Dad was a bricklayer and an active member of the Amalgamated Union of Building Trade Workers (AUBTW) since he had joined at the age of 16 in 1928. When the Amalgamated Society of Painters and Decorators and the Amalgamated Society of Woodworkers merged with the AUBTW in the early 1970s to form the Union of Construction, Allied Trades and Technicians (UCATT), Dad remained active in the new union until he passed away at the age of 80 in 1992. His father, my grandfather, had also been a bricklayer and was a member of the AUBTW's predecessor, the Operative Bricklayer's Society (OBS) which he had joined in 1901. Unfortunately, I never got to meet my Grandad as he passed away before I was born.

Dad had four brothers, my uncles, who were all trade union members. Laurie was a painter and decorator and lived in Glasgow. Like Dad, he was a CPGB member and was very active in the Amalgamated Society of Painters and Decorators. His brother Harold, who lived in Dagenham, was a carpenter and joiner, was a member of the Labour Party and was active in the Amalgamated Society of Woodworkers. He was a branch officer for many years. Dad's other two brothers, Jack and Eric, were both office workers and trade union members. Neither of them was particularly active or militant though. In fact, Eric was a middle-class right-wing snob and was a *Daily Mail* reader who looked down on manual workers. It was always difficult to figure this out, being as both my Grandparents on my father's side had been radical socialists. Indeed, the whole family was steeped in radical traditions.

Between the wars, Dad had worked for many private companies. Early in his career as a bricklayer he worked on the construction of the giant *Ford* factory in the town. He was eventually threatened with violence and run off the site as a supposed 'union troublemaker' by a 'goon squad' of agents who had been hired by the *Ford Motor Company* and charged with the responsibility of union-busting; a practice that had been common in the United States since the 19th century. They were all American thugs and he thought that they were probably working for the *Pinkerton National Detective Agency*; a very well-known union-busting agency in the States who were not averse to using extreme levels of violence against trade unionists.

He also worked on the construction of the giant Becontree estate in Dagenham; 27,000 council homes on over 3000 acres of land housing nearly 100,000 people, mainly from the East End slums, but also from other deprived parts of Britain. In fact, many people migrated from Ireland to Dagenham. This was the first estate to be built on Fordist production line techniques with railway tracks running all around the estate taking Belgium building materials straight from Dagenham Dock and unloading them behind the scaffolding on the site. Although it had been conceived in 1909, building started in 1921 as part of the promise of 'homes fit for heroes' after the terrible suffering experienced by troops in the First World War. Literally hundreds of bricklayers, carpenters and other building trades were employed to complete the project by July 1935. Dad worked on the latter stages of the project and always said that the standard of workmanship expected of workers on the site was very high.

Each dwelling, finished to exacting standards and similar specifications, cost between £250 and £350 to build. They all had indoor bathrooms and toilets; a novelty and a luxury for many new residents from the slums of the East End and elsewhere. They had front and back gardens, with privets across the front of the front gardens. There were municipal parks with gardens carefully laid out and tended by council employed gardeners. The estate was also designed so that there were shops and a pub within a mile of each dwelling. When they married, Mum and Dad were lucky enough to secure the tenancy of one of those council houses in Talbot Road where they remained for the rest of their lives.

In its day it was a very modern and futuristic looking estate. It was and it remains the largest social housing project in the world! In that respect it is unique and should be regarded as one of the wonders of the modern world. Being almost wholly working-class, for many years John Parker, Labour MP for Dagenham from 1945 until he retired in 1983, had the largest majority of any sitting Labour MP in England; despite the fact that he wasn't exactly the most active of MPs. Nevertheless, Conservative candidates at elections would frequently lose their deposits.

Socialist and trade union traditions were brought to the town from all over the country and such commitments were very strong in the area. Most large factories and other workplaces were unionised; none more so than the giant Ford factory employing 75,000 workers. At Ford's there was a very strong and militant shop stewards committee, many of whom were left Labour and Communist Party members. This is also the place where the contemporary struggle against sex discrimination and for equal pay for women really took off with the strike by upholstery workers in 1968, as immortalised in the film *Made in Dagenham* (Cole, 2010). So, this is the social environment in which I was raised.

Dad did work for other private contractors before the war, one being a company called *M. J. Gleeson* from whom he got the sack for trying to organise the workers into the union on one of their sites. *M. J. Gleeson* were to feature heavily in the Fawbert family history of trade union struggles many years later; but more about that in due course! I have to emphasise that Dad was not discriminated against by this or any other company on the basis of his work as a bricklayer, his timekeeping or his productivity.

Dad was an excellent bricklayer and, being ambidextrous, he could lay bricks from either direction, making him one of the fastest and most skilled bricklayers in Dagenham. It's not just me saying that out of family pride; other bricklayers who I worked with later on, such as a lovely old brickie called Dave Banham, told me this. Indeed, he worked on some prestigious projects during the 1930s, including the building of the *London Hilton* and restoration work on the Tower of London. He told me that he was actually rather disappointed at the poor standard of work that was expected at the latter site. The attitude of his contracting employers on that site will be familiar to you, the reader, if you have read Robert Tressell's inspirational book *The Ragged Trousered Philanthropists* (1914) and his account of the attitude of building employers, which was to 'just chuck it up anyhow as fast as you can, so we can make more profit!'

Dad never gave me much advice on becoming an active trade unionist unless I asked for it, but one thing that I do remember him impressing on me was to make sure that I was always a good timekeeper, had as little time off as possible and particularly that I was very good and productive at my chosen trade. He said 'Don't ever give them that excuse (that you are the opposite of those things) to sack you!'

Following demobilisation in 1946 Dad got a job as a bricklayer in the Direct Works Department of Dagenham Council. He later became a foreman and then a General Foreman. He remained with them when they amalgamated with Barking Council in 1965 and stayed with them until he retired in 1977. As a General Foreman in charge of sites, his attitude was very different to that of most of those site agents that he had met that were in charge of sites in the private sector. He insisted that anyone employed either directly or indirectly on his sites was employed under the terms of the National Working Rule Agreement between employers and trade unions and that they were all trade union members. Whilst he ensured that as much work as possible was done by direct employees of the council, if specialist work had to be sub-contracted out, those sub-contractors all had to be employed properly and had to be trade union members.

Occasionally, sub-contractors would attempt to bribe him to overlook the fact that their workers were not trade union members or that they were not directly employed; a common practice in the construction industry. They always got short shrift from Dad and quickly found themselves removed from the site. Dad always worked closely with the shop stewards representing the workers on his sites and it showed how co-operation between workers and management could result in the building of high-quality buildings at a reasonable cost. Unlike most General Foremen in the private sector, Dad preferred to socialise with the lads both on and off the site, eating with them in the site canteen and frequently going for a drink with them after work. He proudly boasted that he had never sacked anyone, preferring to help them improve their skills or their performance.

In the latter years of his career with the council, the Direct Labour Department was run down, as was the case with many local authorities, and Dad was transferred to working out of the council offices as a consultant. He hated it. Although the council office staff were all trade union members, mostly members of the National Association of Local Government Officers (NALGO), he found that many of them had a snobbish, petty-bourgeois attitude, thinking of themselves as a cut-above manual workers.

One incident summed up his disdain for them. When he had worked on site and someone had retired, he used to have a whip-round to buy them a leaving present. The standard contribution from most building workers was £5; not an inconsiderable sum in the 1970s. When he had a whip-round for someone retiring in the offices, people were putting in sixpence or a shilling (two and a half pence and five pence respectively in new money) and were even begrudging that. He was disgusted at their meanness! It was little everyday acts like this that, for Dad, marked out what solidarity, or lack of it, with your fellow workers really meant.

Dad also held many lay positions in the union during his lifetime. He was secretary of the Barking and Dagenham branch of the AUBTW and UCATT until he retired, after which he became branch chairman. Throughout the post-war years, until his retirement, Dad was elected as a delegate to the union's National Delegate Conference that was held in a different region biennially, usually at seaside resorts. When we were children, my brother and me used to go with my Mum and Dad for the week to the conference resort and enjoy a seaside holiday whilst Dad was in the conference hall.

It was one of the only ways that we could afford a holiday as expenses were paid by the union for delegates and their wives (N.B. At that time virtually all delegates were married men). I still have some of the reports of those conferences which include transcripts of all the proceedings. Dad was a frequent and eloquent speaker on many subjects as diverse as deduction of union contributions from source by employers to opposition to the war against the Vietnamese people by the USA. At the time, the USA were trying to drag Britain into their imperialist adventure in that part of South-East Asia. Similarly, Dad was also elected by his union as one of their delegates to the annual TUC conference for 25 consecutive years; a record for his union.

As secretary of the Dagenham branch of the AUBTW, Dad would also take on the responsibility of representing his members in other ways, such as at industry tribunals. This was in the days before ACAS and the Industrial Tribunals legislation for all workers. He would often work on preparing cases for days and sometimes be up all night preparing a case for a tribunal on the following day. All this work was, of course, *pro bono* or free of charge. He did achieve considerable amounts of compensation for many of his members because of his diligence and dedication. Most of his members were very appreciative of all that he did for them, as many older bricklayers that I worked with years later told me, but some were not.

I can remember on one occasion that he worked for days and days on a case and managed to secure quite a tidy sum in compensation for one of his members. When the worker came round to collect his cheque from Dad, he simply took it and said something like 'and about time too!' He didn't even say thank you for all that dad had done. As I said earlier, Dad didn't give me much advice unless I asked for it, but when I first became a shop steward he simply said: 'Remember one thing; however well you do, don't ever expect to get any bouquets for what you do for your members because you won't get any!' I think this was when he was in one of his more pessimistic moods, because he was usually quite optimistic; Communist Party members had to be!

Dad also frequently organised social events, often in the hall at the Fanshawe Tavern in Dagenham, to honour long-serving members of the union where he and others, such as the London Regional Secretary of the union, would make speeches before handing out long-service medals to members who had 25/50 years membership of the union. Besides a raffle, there would be a band and sometimes Dad, and less frequently Mum, would get up on stage and sing a few songs after they'd had a bevvy or two. Once, I remember Mum giving a wonderful rendition of one of her favourite songs, *Danny Boy*, at a union presentation and dance at the Fanshawe.

After he retired from work, Dad was approached by a neighbour who was the secretary of the *Floor and Wall Tilers Association*, a small trade union of just 150 members nationwide, and asked if he would act as their treasurer on a voluntary basis. Dad was only too happy to oblige free of charge. Unfortunately, as I said earlier, Dad passed away at the age of 80 in 1992 from respiratory diseases caused by a lifetime of heavy smoking. Dozens of his comrades from the labour movement attended his funeral and cheered loudly when I talked about his commitment to trade unionism in a eulogy that I gave from the pulpit.

So, my own lifelong commitment to trade unionism and socialist values has to be seen in the context of my upbringing and in particular the influence of my father, but also the influence of my mother who shared his values. The social environment in which I was raised in Dagenham, the largest working-class social housing estate in the world, also contributed greatly to my trade union and socialist commitments. Indeed, we are all, to a greater or lesser extent, prisoners of our social milieu and socialisation, particularly by family, but a lot of thought went into trying to follow in Dad's footsteps.

Chapter 2

An apprenticeship in trade unionism.

I left school at the age of 16 in 1964 and for the summer I worked for a catering company in a tower block of offices at Mansion House. I helped to clean and fill the coffee/tea machines on all 18 floors as well as working in the kitchen doing simple tasks, such as making scotch eggs (I was sick of the sight of them by the time I left there!) and washing and wiping up. It was temporary until I could start a job that would give me a skill. As I had done well at woodwork at school and I really enjoyed it, I wanted to go into a job where I could practice a craft using wood. Dad was against me going into the building trade as a carpenter and joiner and wanted something more highly skilled for me. With Dad's help, in the Autumn, I started as a trainee patternmaker at the *General Engineering Company* in Roebuck Road in Hainault. There, in the patternmaking department, they made precision moulds for aircraft parts working in thousands of an inch. It was, indeed, highly skilled work.

However, I didn't like the job. I was given a lot of menial tasks, rather than being taught the skills I had expected to learn. Later in life, I came to appreciate that that is how all new apprentices/trainees are treated. If I was given any woodworking to do at all, it was usually simple, boring tasks that the patternmakers didn't want to do themselves. Even then, as I had no tools of my own to start with, I had to borrow any tools I needed from an older trainee who was, understandably, very precious about his tools and only let me use them reluctantly. It got to the point where I didn't want to ask him anymore.

Although I was sent to Rush Green College on day release one day a week, it was for an engineering course that taught metalworking skills; something that I wasn't particularly interested in. Also, the pay was £4 2s 6d. After stoppages I got £3 10s 0d in my brown wage packet at the end of the week. Out of that I had to pay Mum £1 2s 6d for my housekeeping and £1 2s 6d repayments on my new *Lambretta* scooter. That left me with the princely sum of just one pound for the week!

So it was that in late 1964, Norman Brown, who I played football with, said that he was working just round the corner in Fowler Road in Hainault at a company called *Durable Suites* as a trainee wood machinist and that there was a vacancy for a trainee cabinet maker there at £6 a week! I jumped at the chance, applied immediately and got the job. When I told Dad what I'd done, he was really annoyed, saying that I'd given up the chance to become a highly-skilled worker in favour of a trade that was not as skilled and that was rapidly being de-skilled even further. In hindsight, he was right of course, but the inability of a 16-year-old working-class lad to defer gratification was a stronger incentive.

Durable Suites made bedroom furniture and was one of two companies that had the same owners and that shared the factory. Mr Saxby was the owner, although he relinquished some of his authority to his two sons, Michael and David. The company had relocated from Green Lanes in the East End and the owners were Jewish, as most East End furniture makers were at that time. The other company was *BT Wood Products* that made highly polished oak and walnut dashboards and internal trim for high-end cars. It was here that I got my first practical lessons in active trade unionism.

Norman worked in the machine shop for *Durable Suites* on the back end of a drum sander, turning over and passing panels back to the feeder to be put through the machine again. I was initially put on the back end of an edging machine in the machine shop stacking the work as it came through after the edges had been glued on. The worker up front, who was responsible for setting up and feeding the machine as well as making sure that the edging went on correctly, was a cabinet maker called Johnny who was probably in his late 20s. Johnny was a biker who I suppose could best be described as a 'petrol head'. He frequently lost his temper when the machine played up, throwing things around and attacking the spoilt panels with any tools that he could get his hands on. I kept right out of the way!

The machine shop was very noisy and dangerous. The workers there used to say that someone was not a proper wood machinist until they had lost at least half a finger; something that happened to Norman's older brother, Colin, while I was there. Quite sensibly, he subsequently gave up the trade and became an insurance salesman! Also, while I was there, a spindle that hadn't been tightened properly flew off across the workshop, cutting the side of a wood machinist's neck on the other side of the workshop. One inch to the left and it would have killed him. Such were the days before the *Health and Safety at Work Act (1974)* and its numerous regulations.

The foreman, simply known as 'Bomber', wore a white coat as all the forcmen did and he was a tyrant. On one occasion a worker hit him and was sacked. Immediately, the whole workshop walked out in protest. The union organiser, a firebrand communist called Jim Kooyman, was called in to investigate. Not only was Jim a firebrand but also, he was a very good organiser who carried out a meticulous investigation, taking statements from witnesses and so on. He produced a mountain of evidence that the foreman had systematically been persecuting this worker for some time and had pushed him over the edge. Kooyman got the man reinstated and the foreman was disciplined by the company. The foreman was rather less tyrannical after that!

Both companies were 'closed shops'; that is that to work there on the shop floor you had to be a member of one of the recognised trade unions. There were two recognised trade unions. Cabinet makers were all members of the National Union of Furniture Trade Operatives (NUFTO), whilst the wood machinists were members of the Amalgamated Society of Woodcutting Machinists. Given my family history, I had no problem with joining NUFTO when asked to do so. I still have that first union card and I've been a trade union member continuously ever since, transferring unions as I changed occupations. The attitude of trade unionists then to the 'closed shop' was that why should they have to work with any worker who reaped the benefits of trade union strength but would not contribute to the collective effort; a view that I shared. Of course, later on under Thatcher's Tory government, the closed shop was made illegal.

The NUFTO branch was in a hall at Seven Kings and it was open one evening a fortnight. They didn't hold meetings, as they should have done, but you could go there to pay your dues. Like many workers, I was often in arears, but impending card inspections at work were often a great incentive to go to the branch to pay up those arears! At that time, as a teenager, I was committed to being a trade union member, but not committed enough to be active in the union. I was more interested in football, girls, popular music, mod fashion and my scooter.

DELEGATES, WIVES AND FAMILIES.

AUBTW delegates, wives and children at the National Delegate Conference in 1970 at Whitley Bay. Mum and Dad are in the middle a couple of rows back.

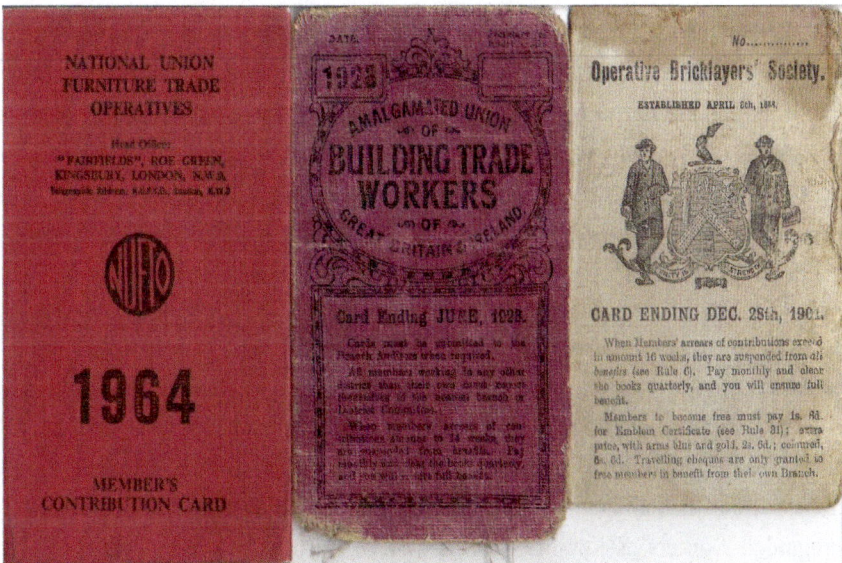

My first union card (1964), my dad's first union card (1928) and my Grandad's first union card (1901).

After a few weeks at the factory, I was transferred into the cabinet making shop and for most of the next four years I was deployed making up wardrobe bottoms, affixing the back and front plinths as well as fixing drawer runners and plastic fixing blocks for the bottoms to be connected to the sides of the wardrobes. By now I was on the bonus scheme and I had to produce roughly 100 wardrobe bottoms each day to make my money. As Dad had said, it was semi-skilled work at best. Nevertheless, the company, in an effort to demonstrate the legitimacy of my 'traineeship', allowed me one day off a week to attend Rush Green College again, but this time to do a woodworking course. After three years, I passed my City and Guilds examination in woodwork and was allowed to stay on for a further year to take, and pass, my Advanced City and Guilds in building craft.

Back at the factory, although what each worker earned in bonus was, in theory, confidential, there was a tacit agreement amongst all the cabinet makers not to go above a certain level of bonus because this might give the company a reason to re-time operations, thinking that the targets were 'too easy' to reach. However, one time it was discovered by one of the newer workers that a long-serving employee called George, who made up the headboards, was earning bonuses far in excess of these agreed maximum limits and had been doing so for some time.

Harry, the shop steward was pressured into calling a shop meeting to discuss this. The longer serving workers admitted that they'd known this, but had allowed George to be an exception. It was made crystal clear to them and George by several workers, especially the newer ones who were seasoned trade unionists anyway, that this was unfair and uncomradely and that he had to fall in line with the rest of the shop because he was jeopardising everyone else's income. George had no alternative but to comply with this view. I had learnt a basic lesson in the strength of collectivism.

As I said, the owner of the company was Mr Saxby. He was rarely seen on the shop floor, but he was well-known to some of the older workers who had worked for him for years. His son Michael was occasionally seen on the shop floor, but he didn't take a great deal of interest in the day-to-day operations of the company. The other son, David, was a different kettle of fish altogether. He was an over-privileged, arrogant, loathsome tyrant who regarded workers as low-life. An example of his attitude was when a *BT Wood Products* worker had a heart attack and before the man had even been taken to hospital, the first thing David asked when he came down on the shop floor was 'Has anybody clocked him out yet?'!

A similar thing happened with regard to the foreman of the cabinet shop in the *Durable Suites* half of the factory where I worked. The foreman was Les, an oily 'company man' who gave total commitment to the firm. 'Taking the white coat' to become a foreman meant relinquishing trade union membership and all loyalty to the workers in favour of an obsequious level of servility to the company and its bosses. In other words, he was a crawler who fawned over the bosses! One new worker there, Sid, an older and very experienced cabinet maker, used to sing all day long and any time Les walked past him he would sing *The Red Flag* with the words changed to 'the working-class can kiss my arse, I've got the foreman's job at last' and laugh his head off! They couldn't sack him or discipline him for singing. After all, as I said, he was a very good cabinet maker and worker and with a strongly unionised workforce, they didn't dare trying to do so.

Anyway, nearer to the end of my time at *Durable Suites*, the foreman Les had a stroke at work. He was taken to hospital and, while he was still in hospital, David told an office worker to 'Send him his cards. He won't be any use to us now.' Although the office workers weren't unionised, the office worker concerned was a good man, was disgusted at David's attitude and sympathetic to workers on the shop floor and so he passed on the information to us. Such was the more evident class divide then and the inhumane attitude of employers.

David would frequently come down on the shop floor throwing his weight around and interfering in the production process. On one occasion, a new screwing machine that didn't need the operative to pick up screws because they would automatically feed in front of the screwdriver one by one, was playing up. David took off his coat, took off his watch, rolled up his sleeves and plunged his hands into the machine to try to fix it. As usual, he just made it worse. So, he gave up, rolled his sleeves back down, put his coat back on and then couldn't find his very expensive, slimline watch.

He walked around the shop accusing everyone of stealing it, until he realised that he'd put it in his coat pocket! He just laughed and never apologised to any of the workers that he had accused of being thieves. His attitude seemed to be that all working-class people are thieves anyway, so why should one false accusation matter. It was already the case that if he tried to interfere on the shop floor with *BT Wood Products* employees, they would all immediately down tools and walk out. No such agreement existed amongst the *Durable Suites* workers.

It was in this context that, on another occasion, Jack Gould, who was a very experienced cabinet maker and trade unionist, but who was fairly new to *Durable Suites*, was working on putting together the carcasses of a new wardrobe line next to my bench. David snatched his saw out of his hand, bearing in mind that these were Jack's own tools, and said 'that's not how I want it done. I want it done like this!' Jack didn't say anything, but I could see the anger in his face. He did no more than turn back to his bench, packed all his tools away in his toolbox including his saw that he snatched back from David and, with toolbox in hand, walked towards the door shouting across the shop floor as he went 'well, I'm not putting up with this anymore and if you lot have got any guts, neither will you!'

The whole shop floor followed him. A meeting, chaired by Harry, the shop steward, was held outside in the yard and it was agreed that nobody would go back until David was banned from the shop floor. After negotiations with David's father, a compromise was reached. It was agreed that David could still visit the shop floor, but that anything he wanted doing by workers had to be communicated through the foreman. I think David's behaviour was partly a consequence of his entitled upbringing but also, I was convinced, that he had mental health problems.

Indeed, I heard many years later that he had a complete mental breakdown. Nevertheless, these experiences at *Durable Suites* helped to cement a belief in me in the value of trade union collective action to defend workers' rights. Although much older than me, Jack Gould was to become a very good friend and confidante; he and his wife also came to my wedding.

After four years and having successfully completed my Advanced City and Guilds in woodwork, I'd had enough of *Durable Suites*. My childhood friend, Ray Pugh, who was brought up in the next street to mine and had worked on the bench opposite me for almost as long as I'd been there, had already left some time earlier. He was working with another old childhood friend called Terry Marquis, who was also a cabinet maker, at a smaller furniture-making firm called *Quinn's*. *Quinn's* had their factory in the old *Sterling Engineering Company's* premises in Dagenham East. *Sterling* was an arms manufacturer that was famous for making the 'Sterling sub-machine gun' amongst other assault rifles during the second world war. Anyway, Ray told me that they were looking for another cabinet maker. So, I applied, got the job and left *Durable Suites* in 1968.

I was only there a few weeks and was unhappy that, despite it being a smaller operation, it was still largely based on a production line. I saw an advertisement in the newspaper for a 'shopfitter'. The pay was 12 shillings an hour; 50 per cent more than I was getting. As I now had my Advanced City and Guilds in Building Craft, I naively thought 'I can do that'. So, I applied, got the job and worked on fitting out a shop in Muswell Hill. I was only there a few weeks when the shop was finished and I was told that I was being made redundant because there was no more work for me with the firm.

At the time, Dad was the General Foreman in charge of the construction of a reception centre on the Gascoigne estate in Barking, working for *Barking and Dagenham Council*. He offered me a job on the site as a carpenter. *Barking and Dagenham* Direct Works Department was a closed shop and my NUFTO union card was considered acceptable by the carpenter shop steward as it was a woodworking craft union. I was there for three months. When the job was winding down, I was transferred to a site where the council were building flats and maisonettes. I was there for just a couple of weeks before I was sacked for not coming up to scratch. Dad was furious, but I was even more furious with myself for being too blasé about my need to manage the switch from factory-based cabinet making to building site carpentry work. I resolved there and then that I would work my guts out to greatly improve my skill set as well as my tool kit to become a first-class worker and carpenter and joiner and to make Dad proud of me.

In early 1969 I saw an advert in the paper for carpenters to work for the *Greater London Council* (GLC) on the maintenance of council houses on the Becontree estate in Dagenham. At the time the GLC owned all of the houses on the Becontree estate. I applied and got the job. Most of my fellow workers were older building workers who had had enough of gallivanting around the country working in poor and dangerous conditions on sites. They were also a great bunch of supportive lads who gave me lots of help and advice on improving my skill set and tool kit. I'd make replacement casement and sash windows as well as doors of all types in the workshop before going out to fit them as well as doing other minor repairs to council houses on the estate.

When I started, I worked out of the Parsloes Avenue depot for three months. One middle-aged worker there called Stan was the shop steward and he was particularly helpful to me. It taught me that being an active trade unionist meant helping your fellow workers in ways other than negotiating better wages and conditions of employment for them.

I was then transferred to the Valence Road depot where, once again, all my fellow workers were very supportive. In particular, there was a very openly gay carpenter called Bill. Being openly gay was very unusual in those days because homosexuality had only just been decriminalised, homophobia was still widespread, sometimes vicious, and 'queer-bashing', as it was known, was commonplace. Bill was not only gay but also loved drag as well as being very camp when he wanted to be. With regard to the latter, this was usually when interacting with the foreman who was extremely homophobic and Bill enjoyed winding him up.

Bill was also the union shop steward. He took me under his wing and helped me enormously. Before you think it, there was never any impropriety as he knew that I was heterosexual and was planning to marry and he was an honourable man. I stayed there for six months. When I got married in September 1969, me and my wife Sue, who was to become my life-long partner, moved to Aveley. There was a GLC maintenance depot at nearby South Ockendon serving the council houses in South Ockendon and Aveley. I applied for and was granted a transfer to the South Ockendon depot where I continued working and honing my skills.

Again, it was a closed shop for all workers in the depot. There were half a dozen maintenance carpenters, all nearing retirement. The shop steward was Frankie Thompson who, along with his labourer 'Scotty', did all the gate and fencing repairs. Frankie was a smashing bloke who loved growing roses and loved his brass band music even more. He suggested to me that it was about time that I transferred my union membership from NUFTO to the Amalgamated Society of Woodworkers (ASW). He invited me to come along to the next branch meeting where he would propose me to the meeting. At that time the ASW was an 'exclusive' rather than an 'inclusive' trade union; in other words, it was one where you had to prove your eligibility to join. It was a direct descendant of the mid-19th century conservative craft unions, who regarded themselves as the 'aristocracy of labour' in that they were very protective of their highly skilled privileges over unskilled labour.

In some industries, branches are based on workplaces and branch meetings take place in those workplaces; sometimes during working time. However, in construction, because of the transient nature of workplaces, it is impractical to base branches at workplaces. So, they are based on towns or districts of cities. Meetings of the ASW South Ockendon and

Aveley branch were held fortnightly in the community hall of the old peoples' bungalows on the South Ockendon estate. There were roughly 125 members in the branch and meetings regularly attracted about 25 of them (Oh, that we got that level of attendance today!).

Frankie proposed my application to join, someone seconded the proposal and then I had to explain why I wanted to join. I was then sent out of the room while the branch members discussed my application. In theory, it was also a secret society; a consequence of the long history of the persecution of trade unionists going back to the 'Tolpuddle Martyrs' and beyond. After five minutes, I was asked back into the meeting and was informed by the Branch Secretary, Ted Childs, that my application to join and transfer from NUFTO had been accepted 'subject to Bridlington'. The Bridlington Principles were a set of, now defunct, TUC rules to prevent unions from poaching members from other unions. I was then given a round of applause.

Many members of the branch, including the Secretary Ted Childs, were fairly conservative in their views i.e. leaning towards the right of the Labour Party. One regular attender at branch meetings was even a member of the organisation 'Conservative Trade Unionists'; an oxymoron if ever there was one! Since the years of attacks by the Tories on the trade union movement, starting with the Thatcher government, and as their membership has dwindled as a result, they have now changed their name to 'Conservatives at Work'. However, this 'Conservative' member was almost universally regarded as an outsider and not in tune at all with the mood of the branch. Also, there were many branch members who were much more left-leaning, including the chairman, Ken and my shop steward Frankie.

Many of the members of the branch, however, regarded the ASW as more of a 'friendly society' that was there to provide support and benefits for members as well as, or sometimes rather than, acting like a traditional trade union. Although this made them less militant, there were some positives to this culture. For example, when a member of the branch passed away, Ted, the branch secretary, on behalf of the branch, would always get a wreath for the funeral, attend the funeral with another member and also offer financial support to the widow from branch funds. Later, Ted would visit the widow and offer to auction the deceased member's tools at a branch meeting. A considerable sum would usually be raised for the widow. Whilst the union wasn't particularly militant then, these kinds of attitudes helped me to appreciate more fully what solidarity amongst working people really meant.

Back at the depot, every morning the foreman, Bill Bailey, would first ask if anyone had any job tickets still not completed from the previous day before handing out enough job tickets for what he thought was a day's work to each carpenter. We would then all go out on our council bikes with carriers on the front of them to carry our tools, whilst Bill would drive around the estate in the council van delivering the materials needed for jobs that he had allocated to each of us. We were left alone to get on with it and just had to return to the yard shortly before finishing time to hand in our completed job tickets (unless, of course, we needed to go back for any other reason such as making up some joinery in the workshop or replenishing our supplies of screws, nails etc.) and to sign off for the day.

On top of our nationally agreed basic pay, there was an individual bonus scheme. There was a booklet of timings for each operation, but what each carpenter earned was as much down to how 'creative' they could be in how they described what they had done on the back of each job ticket as it was to the amount of work that they had actually done. You couldn't lie of course as a sample of your jobs would be checked by a bonus clerk, but how you reported what you'd done could often make all the difference. I almost always managed to earn the maximum bonus allowed of £9 2s 6p each week; a considerable sum on top of the basic wage at that time. As Sue was also working full-time at Corringham, most days I managed to get home early to get the dinner prepared, just returning to the depot to sign off.

Conflict was rare during my three years there and if there was any, it was usually over issues between individuals. On one occasion, I was given a job ticket to go to one house. When I arrived there the house was absolutely filthy. Most tenants took great care to look after their council houses/flats, but this one was not only filthy but also there was excrement everywhere from their German Shephard dog; even all over the living room carpet! I made an excuse to the tenant that I had to go back to the yard to get some screws.

When I returned to the yard, I gave the job ticket back to the foreman, Bill, saying that I refused to work in such an environment. He said 'you know I could sack you for refusing to do a job, don't you?' I said 'I don't care. I'm not working in that s***hole!' I was getting ready to call in my shop steward, Frankie Thompson, when Bill replied 'Fair enough. Leave it with me.' Fair play to him; he went round to the house, inspected it and told the tenant that he wouldn't send any of his carpenters back there until she had cleaned the place up. I, nor anyone else to my knowledge, ever went back to the house.

Another incident taught me a valuable lesson about the benefit of using local authority direct labour for council house repairs. There was a sense of providing a good service for tenants amongst the directly employed lads as much as just 'doing a job'. When visiting older tenants, for example, workers would have a cup of tea and a chat with them, especially if they were on their own. They would do other little jobs for them, such as changing light bulbs, even though this was outside the remit of their job tickets. 'Looking after' tenants was the over-riding priority, not making money.

As I said earlier, Frankie Thompson and his mate Scotty were responsible for doing fencing and gate repairs. They were always careful when renewing chestnut fencing in the back gardens to look after the tenants' plants and flowers and to do as little damage to them when they were next to fences as possible. Frankie would even prune tenants' roses if need be. However, as the estates were getting older, more and more of the fencing needed replacing and Frank and Scotty couldn't cope with the increasing demand. So, the council decided to bring in a sub-contractor working on a fixed price to renew the fencing along the back gardens of whole streets of terraced housing. When they'd finished it looked like they'd driven a Sherman tank across the back gardens of whole streets to clear the old fencing, which they had left in piles on the corner greens! Council employees were left to clear up the mess.

As mentioned earlier, in 1970/1971, following a series of mergers, the ASW joined forces with the Amalgamated Society of Painters and Decorators and the Amalgamated Union of Building Trade Workers to form the Union of Construction, Allied Trades and Technicians (UCATT). This was to prove to be a significant development in uniting building workers in a common cause, as we shall see. It brought together in one union over a quarter of a million trade unionists. Although the new union was mostly still for skilled workers, it became more of an 'inclusive' rather than an 'exclusive' trade union.

By 1972 I had been working for the GLC maintenance department for three years and, whilst I was reasonably contented with the job, Sue and I were still finding it a bit of a struggle to manage to meet our financial commitments, especially the mortgage payments. Behind our back garden was an alleyway and on the other side of the alleyway was an old disused factory unit that was taken over by a guy called Roy Pearce. Roy turned it into a joinery workshop where he, three employees and an apprentice would make up bespoke joinery before taking it out to sites to fit. I got talking to Roy over the fence one day and he asked me if I'd like to come and work for him. He offered National Working Rule Agreement wages and conditions as well as a bonus that was equivalent to what I was already getting. The difference was that he was also offering a lot of overtime; something that was not available at my council job.

I took up his offer and for a few months I worked in the workshop as well as going out in the company van to do work on a car showroom in Chadwell Heath, a hospital in Stratford, East London and Warley Hospital, a psychiatric infirmary in Brentwood. Much of the time I worked with Frank, an older carpenter/joiner who I got on really well with. With me being a life-long atheist, I didn't much like the 'foreman' who stayed in the workshop all the time. He was a bit of a 'bible-basher' and a strict disciplinarian to boot. Roy, though, was a decent bloke to work for, although I did walk into his office unannounced one day and caught him licking and sticking dozens of stamps to everyone's holiday cards. N.B. This was supposed to be done weekly, but Roy made some lame excuse for why he'd 'got a bit behind' and assured me that it wouldn't happen again. Such were the problems of working for a small business at the time; problems that also arose frequently with sub-contractors.

Since leaving *Durable Suites* in 1968, I'd kept in contact with a few of the people I had worked with there. One of them was Bert Woods from Basildon. Bert had been at my wedding and had taken a cine film of the whole event. Bert contacted me and said that he was now working for *Ashby and Horner*, a prestigious joinery company that can trace its origins back to 1690. They made high quality, bespoke joinery in their factory at West Thurrock. Bert said that they were looking for experienced joiners and encouraged me to apply. I did so, was interviewed by the foreman, Derek, and started work there in late 1972. There were about 20 joiners and five apprentices in the workshop at the time.

It was, once again, National Working Rule Agreement wages and conditions as well as a company 'profit-sharing scheme', although nobody ever seemed to know how a share of the profits was worked out! There was also a significant amount of overtime available because the company could never find enough joiners who possessed the considerable skills needed to do the high-quality work that the job demanded. One example is that while I was there, the company had a contract to make and deliver several very high-quality doors to Abu Dhabi for the Sheikh's palace. The company even had to make specially designed crates to send them in. There was a deadline that had to be reached to make certain flights from Heathrow. Joiners had to work 24 hours a day all weekend to meet the deadline. The amount of overtime worked was later to prove to be an effective weapon in the battle for improved wages and conditions.

It was a closed-shop and the shop steward was a quiet but popular and shrewd leader called Mervyn. Shortly after I started there, another joiner was taken on who refused to join the union, in his words 'on religious grounds'. This was a spurious reason. At that time there was only one major religious grouping in the UK that objected to their members joining trade unions and that was the *Plymouth Brethren*. TUC advice was that members of the *Plymouth Brethren* should not be made to join a trade union, but that they should have to pay an amount equivalent to trade union subscriptions to a recognised charity. However, this fellow was not a member of the *Plymouth Brethren* and was just trying it on. He was also reminded that at his interview he had been told that if he was taken on, he would have to join the union. So, there was no excuse for him not to join. He left rather than join the union.

It was 1972 and I was becoming increasingly disillusioned with mainstream politics. The Labour governments led by Harold Wilson between 1964 and 1970 had done little to redress the imbalance of wealth and power between the capitalist class and the working-class. Ted Heath's Tory government from 1970 had launched attacks on miners prompting a national strike that was eventually won for the miners by calling for solidarity action at the so-called 'Battle of Saltley Gate'. Over 15,000 workers from nearby engineering factories marched to the picket line on the outskirts of Birmingham to force the police to close the gates on the coke depot. The government caved in and the miners celebrated an historic victory.

During that period, five dockers were also arrested and imprisoned by the newly created National Industrial Relations Court for refusing to obey a court order to stop picketing a container depot in East London. Their arrest and imprisonment led to a series of strikes until there was virtually an unofficial national strike. The TUC were forced to call a General Strike. As with the miners, the Labour Party hierarchy did little to support the strikers. Led by communist activists, the fight-back resulted in the government caving in and producing someone called 'the Official Solicitor', who only the most ardent follower of politics had ever heard of, to declare that the decision of the court was unlawful. Led by communists, the five dockers were carried shoulder high from Pentonville prison by a crowd of thousands of supporters who had marched from North London. This all finally convinced me of the need for more radical action to secure a change in the balance of wealth and power in favour of working people. I joined the Communist Party of Great Britain (CPGB).

Chapter 3

Becoming more active.

B ack at *Ashby and Horner* there was a works council set up by the company to serve as a conduit between management and workers. Mervyn, the shop steward, asked me if I'd like to represent the joiners on it. I agreed, but quickly discovered that we weren't allowed to discuss wages and conditions of employment. It was no more than a talking shop designed to appease the workers and convince them that they had some interest and involvement in the company's affairs. Nevertheless, I stayed on the council, doing what I could for the workers I represented, mostly with regard to welfare provision.

However, a more significant development was about to take place. The first and only national building workers' strike was about to take off. Under the new union, UCATT, together with the Transport and General Workers Union and the General, Municipal and Boilermakers Union, craft and unskilled building workers united and put in an across-the-board wage claim of £30 for a 35-hour week. At that time the basic rate of pay for skilled workers was just £20 and £17 for labourers for a 40-hour week. In addition, the unions wanted an end to the use of 'the lump'; non-union labour who worked on sites for a lump sum, cash in hand. Lumpers paid no tax, no national insurance, trained no apprentices and were not entitled to holiday or sick pay. This was the 'gig economy' long before we called it the gig economy!

In completely rejecting the claim, the employers were obdurate. Connected by their main negotiating body, the National Federation of Building Trade Employers (NFBTE), the construction companies were powerful and had longstanding links with and contributed large sums of money to the Conservative Party. Many Conservative Ministers and MPs were also Directors of construction companies. They, like most independent commentators, thought that it would be impossible for the unions to launch any effective industrial action in an industry that was so fragmented and transient.

Indeed, the UCATT leadership had already accepted a deal. However, site activists rejected the deal and independently started strike action. Their actions were co-ordinated by a rank-and-file group known as the *Building Workers' Charter* which was led by the carpenter Lou Lewis who was a leading communist. The union hierarchy had misjudged the mood of building workers and were reluctantly forced to support the action. From 26th June 1972 they sanctioned strikes on a selective basis. Each region was instructed to identify roughly ten important sites to strike in their area; ones where employers were vulnerable to time penalties in their contracts. The unions believed that this would put pressure on individual contractors to settle, after which a further group of sites would be brought out on strike.

Employers start to break ranks due to selective strikes.

Building workers on a 'flying picket' during the 1972 dispute.

Other sites and subsidiary workplaces, such as joinery workshops, were asked to ban all overtime. At *Ashby and Horner* Mervyn called a meeting of all the joiners who voted unanimously to stop all overtime. This was devastating for the company who, as I said earlier, were reliant on their workforce doing massive amounts of overtime. Whilst many building sites had stopped work and didn't need joinery supplies, much of the work that *Ashby and Horner* did was not destined for UK building sites. I've already mentioned the doors that were bound for Abu Dhabi. In addition, I was working on constructing a suite of high-quality office furniture for the managing director of *William and Glyn's Bank* for example, whilst other joiners were working on building an oak dais for the Queen's throne to stand on. Many other jobs of this nature were not destined for UK building sites that were on strike.

After a couple of weeks, one of *Ashby and Horner's* directors thought that he would circumvent negotiations with Mervyn, our shop steward. He came down on the shop floor and asked all the joiners to gather round. He asked us to reconsider our decision to ban overtime, reasoning that the dispute really had nothing to do with us, was only hurting our own pockets and could result in the company facing financial difficulties. We all listened intently to his pleas which finished with 'so, will you reconsider the ban on overtime?' One older joiner spoke up and said 'yes, we will…' and while the director was congratulating himself on his powers of oratory and persuasion, the joiner, after a pause, continued '… when you pay us what we're asking for.' Everyone nodded in agreement and the director left red-faced. He had misjudged the mood of the workforce and our support for our shop steward, Mervyn.

Then the management started pinning press cuttings from the *Daily Telegraph* (what I, like others, called the *Daily Torygraph*) onto the Works Council notice board saying how the unions were losing the dispute and how workers were refusing to come out on strike across large swathes of the country. This was all totally untrue propaganda. So, being a member of the Works Council, I started pinning press cuttings of my own taken from the socialist daily newspaper, the *Morning Star*, next to the ones from the *Daily Telegraph*; ones that told the story of what was actually going on across the country – that the strike was spreading and was solid wherever it took hold. After a while, press cuttings from the *Daily Telegraph* stopped appearing on the notice board. So, being a member of the Works Council did have some use after all! Later, I was quietly asked by management to stop pinning press cuttings from the *Morning Star* about the dispute onto the Works Council notice board, as they were deemed to be 'inappropriate'. Strange that no mention was made of *Daily Telegraph* reports on the dispute being pinned to the notice board being 'inappropriate'.

In fact, rank-and-file workers on those sites that had been chosen to strike by the union hierarchy decided to adopt the tactic successfully practiced by the miners in their dispute earlier in the year of using flying pickets; they travelled in cars, and sometimes coaches, to working sites to explain in canteen and outdoor meetings that all building workers were on strike and that all work should stop. At first, they were uncertain whether even union members on other sites would join them. However, not only did union members on other sites enthusiastically agree to join the strike but also many other workers joined one of the recognised unions and were keen to join in the action. The unity and confidence of members grew quickly. By the end of July many workers were not prepared to carry on working and simply pay a levy to support those on strike, as instructed by the UCATT leadership. They wanted to strike too, to maximise the pressure on their employers. When a further improved offer was rejected by members in the first week of August, despite UCATT's leadership declaring that it would be accepted, the unions were forced to declare an all-out strike, but without strike pay.

Co-ordinated by the communist-led *Building Workers' Charter*, the tactic of flying pickets proved very effective. There was virtually a total shutdown of all major building sites in the UK; something that surprised the employers who had thought that such unity and co-ordination was impossible. The level of participation and a common claim for which workers in the industry were fighting had created a strong feeling of unity and solidarity. This was a major achievement in a workforce that was historically fragmented and had previously been divided on craft lines, as I mentioned earlier. After 12 weeks, the strike ended on 18 September. This was after the union negotiators accepted a new offer of a basic rate of £26, a 30% increase, followed by further increases over the following two years.

Many activists opposed the settlement, not least because there was no agreement on eradicating lump labour; a failure that was, in later years, destined to come back to haunt the unions. In Liverpool the strike carried on for a further week, but the overwhelming feeling was that this was still a great victory for building workers. The Conservative Party and the employers, however, were not going to let this pass without punishment. One of the 'Pentonville Five' dockers, Bernie Steer, warned that trade unionists should prepare for a counter-attack from the Tories and their backers. He said:

These people are not finished… they are vicious people and, in my view, they will be like a wounded animal now. They will retreat in a corner; they have had three good wallops [the miners, the dockers and the building workers] and now they are going to start slashing out (Tribune. 2022).

Indeed, the employers were bitter and decided to get their revenge with waves of victimisation and blacklisting. Long after the strike was over representatives of the major contracting companies, Conservative government ministers, senior police officers and members of the security services colluded to charge a number of building workers from the North West with conspiracy to intimidate, affray, and unlawful assembly. This was despite the fact that all those involved in the picketing in that area had been congratulated at the time by police officers on the ground for their impeccable behaviour when visiting other sites to persuade workers to join the strike. The police commanding officer went so far as to shake the hand one of the leading pickets, Des Warren, and congratulate him on the discipline and good humour of the strikers. This counted for nothing. Thirty-five building workers, including Des, were arrested and charged.

Eleven were acquitted at Mold Crown Court after defence lawyers had exercised their right to challenge potential jurors. The remaining twenty-four were all found guilty at Shrewsbury Crown Court after the Lord Chancellor had intervened to abolish the defence's ability to challenge jurors. They became known as the 'Shrewsbury 24'. Twenty-one of the defendants were fined, but John McKinsie-Jones was given a six-month jail sentence, Ricky Tomlinson was given two years in prison and Des Warren was sentenced to three years. As Des Warren said from the dock at the time, the only conspiracy that had taken place was a conspiracy by the capitalist class. He was later proved to be absolutely right. In 2015 Labour MP Andy Burnham revealed to Parliament previously secret files, which indeed showed a government conspiracy to frame and jail the strikers.

Tomlinson was released early, but Warren was made to serve his full sentence. Whilst in prison, he was continually drugged with a cocktail of tranquillisers, colloquially known as 'liquid cosh'. His family and friends are all convinced that it was this treatment that resulted in him contracting Parkinson's Disease and dying at the early age of sixty-six. After the national building workers' strike in 1972, the employers intensified their campaign against socialists and active trade unionists on their sites and began to use the blacklist much more, as I said earlier.

The Economic League, a secret right-wing organisation, set up the so-called 'Services Group' on behalf of its construction clients to keep a list of trade union activists in the building industry that was accessible to employers when they had workers apply for jobs on their sites and to which employers could add new names. I thought that it was important to explain the wider dispute and its aftermath in a bit of detail because the effects were later to prove to become very personal for me.

During my time at *Ashby and Horner*, Bert and me were sent out to fit all the bespoke furniture at the new *War Graves Commission* buildings in Maidenhead. We travelled across London to the site each day for two weeks. The rest of the time, however, I worked in the workshop. A lot of the work was just damping down and rubbing down hardwood components and mouldings. After 18 months I had enough and so had my fingers that were often red raw, cracked and bleeding. I was yearning to get back out on to site work. I saw an advertisement in the local paper for carpenters to second-fix a few hundred houses on a new build council estate in Tilbury for local builders *Walsham and Co.*

I went along with Graham, another joiner from *Ashby and Horner*, and met John Walsham who showed us around the site. He already had a couple of chippies working on the site, but they were on 'the lump'. Both Graham and myself told him that we didn't mind working on piecework, but that we wanted to be directly employed, 'on the cards' as it were, with a guaranteed minimum of National Working Rule Agreement pay and conditions, including holiday pay. He readily agreed. He was desperate for good carpenters and he asked us if we knew of any others who might be interested. When we told everyone back at *Ashby and Horner* three other joiners, Alan, Mick and Johnny, applied and were accepted on the same basis.

Because each finished dwelling was inspected by a Clerk of Works and if there was any 'snagging' to be done, we would not be paid any more until it was done, we were all more or less left alone to get on with it. Houses were loaded up with all the materials we needed by our labourer and we all worked there for a few months. As the site was nearing its finish, most of the other carpenters drifted away to other sites, whilst Graham and myself were asked by John Walsham for a price to fit the hardwood treads and handrails to the dogleg concrete stairs of the several blocks of flats on the site. I negotiated a really good price for what was work that needed good joinery skills. When the staircases on all the flats were nearly completed, I decided it was time to move on. Graham stayed on and I heard that he had later been made up to a foreman on other *Walsham* sites.

I then started on a site in West Ham working directly for *The London Borough of Newham* on a small housing project. It was mostly second-fixing, but there was some first-fixing and roofing. It was a closed-shop, as local authority direct labour departments invariably were; not a problem for me, obviously. The shop steward Stan, a decent man, had been with the council for many years and the foreman, Charlie, was very likeable. There was a collective bonus scheme by trade in operation, but as the work was all 'bitty' and some of the targets were not particularly easy to meet, most weeks the carpenters never earnt much on top of their basic wages. In addition, the payroll department in the council offices in Stratford was clearly in a mess, because virtually every Friday when I got my brown wage packet, they had got my wages wrong; and I wasn't the only one, by any means! This meant a trip to the office for many of us nearly every week to join a queue to sort it out.

Sue and I had just found out that she was pregnant with our first child and quite frankly, I couldn't afford to stay there, much as I got on well with the foreman and all my fellow workers. Together with Johnny and Mick who I had worked with at both *Ashby and Horner* and *Walsham and Co.*, I got a job with *Hammond and Miles* working on a site of 43 new-build houses in Barkingside. It was mostly to second-fix the houses but also there was a small amount of other work such as first-fixing door and window frames, putting in staircases and some roofing. It was once again 'on the cards' working under National Working Rule Agreement pay and conditions. The General Foreman was a reasonable man who just wandered round the site most of the day, making sure that nobody had any problems. The bonus scheme was an individual one and all of us made reasonable money with the targets that we were given.

As it was only 43 houses, the job didn't last long though. With just a few houses left to second-fix, Johnny and Mick left, leaving me to complete the remaining dwellings. Sue and I had our first child, a boy we called Paul. In view of my added responsibilities, I was desperate to find another site before the last five houses were completed. Luckily, Johnny and Mick had got another job on a much larger site in Briar Road, Harold Hill working for the *Greater London Council* (GLC) Direct Labour Department on building 1,200 new homes. They told me that the GLC were looking for more carpenters and that they would recommend me if I applied. I applied and got the job in late 1974. It was mostly first and second-fixing and there were about 30 carpenters amongst the roughly 200-strong workforce.

It was a closed-shop and there was a very active works committee of UCATT and TGWU representatives. Like on many sites, the carpenters worked in pairs. On my first day I was put to work with another new starter. Within minutes of starting to work with this other new starter, he told me that, although it was a closed-shop, he hated trade unions and that he had no intention of joining one. Come break time, I told the foreman, Alan, that I didn't want to work with him and told him the reason why. So, he put me to work with another carpenter called Peter and the other guy was told that he'd have to join UCATT or leave. He chose to leave.

However, I was only working with Peter for a couple of hours when he told me that he was a member of the National Front (NF). He told me that his dad was a long-standing

Labour Party activist and that it really angered his dad that he had joined such a fascist organisation. I couldn't refuse to work with another carpenter, as I was already walking a tightrope. At that time the National Working Rule Agreement stated that an employer could sack a worker in his first week of employment without giving a reason. Trade union activists would usually keep their heads down and not draw attention to themselves in their first week on a new site. To refuse to work with two other carpenters on my first day would have been risky to say the least. So, I kept my mouth shut. I ended up working with Peter for 18 months on that site.

At first, when he made racist remarks, I would either ignore him, shout and scream abuse at him or, more often than not, just take the p**s out of his ignorance. All the workers on the site were white, as workers were on most Essex sites at that time. One day, though, a black carpenter of West Indian origin called Sam was transferred to the site from another GLC site in West London. At first Peter made racist remarks about him being useless, like all black workers. Sam was getting on a bit, so he wasn't quite as quick as some of the younger chippies, but he turned out to be a really good carpenter. This seemed to infuriate Peter as here was living proof that repudiated his racist theories about the inferiority of black workers.

As we had to continue working together, after a while, both Peter and I would avoid any conversation that would lead to conflict and, while we were working, we talked about things like music, fashion, television or films that we had seen. I also felt at times that deep-down, like many youngsters who joined the NF at that time, that he wasn't really a committed fascist and that he was a decent bloke inside who had only joined the NF to wind his dad up. I would like to think that he has since seen the error of his ways and, like the actor Ricky Tomlinson says with regard to himself in his book *Ricky* (2004), put his membership of the National Front down to youthful indiscretion. Indeed, Peter really showed his sensitive side when his Mum passed away and he also sought my advice on relationships when his girlfriend dumped him; me of all people! Nevertheless, we became known to some on the site as 'the odd couple'.

Anyway, the convenor of shop stewards on the site was a very vociferous TGWU scaffolder called Johnny Bowles, but Johnny wasn't the 'brains' behind the decisions of the works committee. Although he liked to give the impression that he was 'in charge', whenever there were difficult decisions to be made, he would always seek the advice of the carpenter shop steward, Pat Tracey; known to many of his friends as 'PJ'. Indeed, when he was asked difficult questions at mass meetings, he would frequently look in Pat's direction, expecting him to give an answer. Pat was quite happy to play this role. Pat was only in his late 30s, but he was a very experienced trade unionist and socialist. He had originally come from the West of Ireland and had worked on some of the major sites in London, including on the Barbican site. He had been a shop steward on the Barbican at the time of the massive unrest in the 1960s that led to a government Committee of Enquiry, the *Cameron Report* (1967), into industrial relations on the Barbican and Horseferry Road sites, and the eventual sacking and blacklisting of all the works committee on the former site.

Pat had since found it extremely difficult to get work on any site until he got a job on this site with the GLC. He thought that this was proof that at least the GLC didn't use the blacklist. He was very much on the left politically and although he expressed a great deal of admiration for communists like Lou Lewis and Max Bear that he had worked with, he was not a member of the CPGB himself because he was a Catholic and couldn't reconcile that with the party's stance on abortion. He also oozed an air of quiet, laid-back confidence. I learnt from Pat that being militant didn't mean ranting and raving all the time; that to be effective as a shop steward you more often than not had to be shrewd and crafty and sometimes even give the impression that you are on the side of management if you wanted to get a good deal for your members.

Anyway, the site was split in two and Pat was working on one side of the site, I was on the other. He suggested that another shop steward for the carpenters needed to be elected for the side of the site that I was on. He obviously had me in mind. A meeting was held and he put my name forward. His nomination was seconded and I was duly elected. The works committee had their own office, a small hut on the site, where we held weekly committee meetings. We would also hold monthly mass meetings for all the workers on the site in the site canteen where Johnny would regale us all with his rhetoric. He was sometimes interrupted by Pat, particularly when he strayed from the policies and actions that we had all agreed at the works committee meetings or when Pat felt that Johnny was digging a big hole for himself.

However, there was one occasion when Pat wasn't there to rescue Johnny. The Labour Party had passed a motion at their annual conference calling for the nationalisation of the construction industry. In response, the employers had set up an organisation called the 'Campaign Against Building Industry Nationalisation' (CABIN). They launched an expensive poster campaign, flew a hot air balloon over the TUC conference and were granted permission by several employers to show anti-nationalisation films on sites. True to form, the employers refused to allow the unions to reply to their case on their sites. So, in November of 1975 UCATT and the TGWU publicly challenged CABIN to an independently chaired debate in London's Conway Hall on the Labour Party's proposals.

Pat and I, along with a number of others from our site, went along to a packed Conway Hall to hear the debate. The employers had done very little preparation and had chosen a series of speakers who clearly had little or no experience of public speaking. In contrast, the unions had planned and organised their strategy extremely well and chosen full time officials and convenor stewards from large sites who were very experienced and able public speakers; apart from Johnny Bowles that is. They even had a couple of academics to give more detailed and scholarly presentations outlining the case for nationalisation of the construction industry. As usual, Johnny's heart was in the right place, but without Pat on stage to support him, he made quite a few gaffs. Johnny's contribution aside, the debate was embarrassingly one sided; as the *Morning Star* said, the employers got 'a drubbing'.

Pat and I also went to a number of meetings of UCATT shop stewards from the local area held at Barking Town Hall. They were meetings that had been set up by the union hierarchy to co-ordinate rank-and-file activity in the separate areas of the London region. The full-time official for the area, a right-winger called Tom Howard, was there as were a few right-wing shop stewards. However, there was a majority of left-wingers there including left-Labour and communist shop stewards such as Jim Franklin, Billy Butler, Larry Spector and Bill O'Shaughnessy. Because of his previous union activity in and around London, Pat already knew most of these lads well. I got to become friends with all of them and to recognise that, despite their ideological differences and different party affiliations, they supported one another like they were family. Indeed, all of them and more came to my dad's funeral when he passed away in 1992.

Going back to the site, there was never any conflict about bonus payments. The incentive scheme was a collective one for each trade and one of the two carpenter foremen, Alan, assured everyone not to worry about how much work we did as he would note down everything and present it to the bonus clerk in such a way as to make sure that we earnt a good bonus every week. I think that this was the case with all the other trades. The major conflict that did take place was the sacking of the painter and decorator shop steward for punching a supervisor. The supervisor was a pretty nasty individual; a bully who frequently lambasted workers and got into rows with them on the site.

The shop steward claimed that after a blazing row with the supervisor, the supervisor had thrown the first punch. He had certainly picked on the wrong guy as the painter shop steward was an ex-professional boxer! They ended up rolling around on the floor before being separated by onlookers. The painters and decorators immediately stopped work and a meeting of all the workers on the site was called where it was decided to strike until the shop steward was reinstated. The site agent was a hard-headed Welshman called Ivor. In a meeting with the works committee, he refused point blank to reinstate the shop steward, saying that such gross misconduct could never be tolerated.

So, the strike went on for about a week until the GLC at County Hall set up an enquiry. Several witnesses to the incident went to County Hall, opposite the Houses of Parliament, and gave evidence that they saw the supervisor throw the first punch. The GLC had no option but to reinstate the shop steward and to reimburse everyone on site for the pay that they had lost during the strike. What happened to the supervisor, I don't know, but he was never seen on site again.

However, the works committee didn't just deal with disputes. We had guest speakers at mass meetings in the canteen, for example. One such speaker that I invited was Jack Henry who had been the convenor steward on the Horseferry Road site which was one of the two sites that was the subject of the government committee of enquiry mentioned earlier; the *Cameron Report* (1967). He became a member of the Executive Council of UCATT and a full-time official. Jack was a fine speaker, but later on there were accusations that he became 'too close' to employers (Smith & Chamberlain, 2016: 254).

The works committee also campaigned over other issues. The GLC had maternity leave provisions in place for council employees, but as the overwhelming majority of site workers were young men, we argued with the council that they should also be providing paternity leave. Ken Livingstone had been elected as a Labour councillor on the GLC in

1973, so we put it to Ken that, as he declared himself to be a 'feminist', that he should support us in this endeavour. Ken agreed and was instrumental in getting an agreement from the council that male council employees would get two weeks' paid leave on the birth of a child to their respective wives. Trade unionists in other workplaces fought for and got similar agreements over the years. As in this case, legislation giving all workers benefits and rights often follow once they have been established as the norm in many trade union organised workplaces.

The works committee didn't just deal with issues that would benefit the workers we represented though. We felt that we needed to show some responsibility to the local community as well. In Harold Hill, there was a centre being built for mentally disabled youngsters to be able to live semi-independent lives, but they needed money to equip the centre with facilities to be able to function effectively. As a works committee we decided to organise a weekly site-wide raffle to raise the money. Within weeks we had raised enough to go as a works committee to the centre to hand over the cheque and to have tea and sandwiches with staff and youngsters who would be resident there. We decided to keep the weekly raffle going to raise money for the Christmas Eve booze-up. At that time building workers usually packed up work at lunchtime on Christmas Eve and went to the pub for the afternoon, as I guess workers probably did in many other industries.

We then requested that we start the party in the site canteen. At first, Ivor, the site agent, refused. After a few more 'discussions', he relented. Then we said that he obviously wouldn't want anyone going out on the site having had too much to drink, as it was dangerous. To cut a long story short, in the end he agreed that as long as workers clocked in, they would be paid for the day and not have to go out on the site. The party and the drinking started in the canteen at 8.00am. By the time the pubs opened at 11.30, most of the workers were very drunk.

Then they adjourned to *The Plough* pub on Gallows Corner in Romford. When I got there I saw that 'Topper', a rather eccentric and larger than life labourer, was strapped to the water wheel in the middle of the pub going round and round to the amusement of everyone, including himself! I walked home from there much the worse for wear. On my way through Romford town centre, I walked past *Woolworth's* where I saw a number of the painters dancing in the shop window! I think the works committee's 'party' had certainly enabled everyone to get a good start to their Christmas break.

After Christmas, several of the works committees of union-organised sites in the East End, including our own, got together to organise a 'Free Des Warren' concert at the *Theatre Royal* in Stratford. Labour had won the General Election in 1974 and had promised to 'look again' at the case of the Shrewsbury 24. However, Roy Jenkins was appointed Home Secretary and, despite the fact that his own coal-miner of a father had been jailed under similar circumstances, he refused to sanction the release of Warren. The rat was later to break away from Labour with Shirley Williams, Bill Rogers and David Owen (known as the 'gang of four') to form the Social Democratic Party which of course later merged with the Liberal Party.

We managed to get a number of local bands and comedians to agree to perform for free at the concert, but we needed somebody to top the bill. One lad on our site said 'oh, I'll ask Long John Baldry if he'll do it.' Nobody believed him because he was thought to be a bit of a 'bullshitter' and Long John Baldry was also a big star who had had a string of hits, including a number one with *Let the Heartaches Begin* in 1967. However, this guy came in the following day with Long John's phone number on a piece of paper. Of course, mobile phones didn't exist then. That evening, Long John was contacted and, after asking a number of questions about what the concert was for, he said that he would be very pleased to do it.

Tickets for the concert were sold out in no time at all and Long John Baldry performed an acoustic set of all his biggest hits at the top of the show. A considerable amount of money was raised for the campaign. Long John must have done a lot of benefit gigs like this one before because he said on stage that his brother was a copper who had said to him 'I keep getting them locked up and you keep doing benefit gigs to get them out!'

In early 1976 the site was rapidly nearing completion. Pat and his family decided to return to Ireland and I was left as the only carpenter shop steward. The bonus clerk had sat in his nice, warm hut working out bonuses from the information that Alan, the foreman, had given him for months now rather than going out on site to check for himself what had been done. As the weather started to improve, he decided to take a tour of the site and was horrified at what he saw! Alan had by this time booked in work three months in advance of what was completed by the 30 or so carpenters! He told Alan that no more bonus would be paid to the carpenters until all the backlog had been cleared. Strangely, the bonus clerk's hut burnt down that night with all his records (there were no copies) going up in smoke! I think it must have been spontaneous combustion!

Nevertheless, some of the carpenters decided that it was time to go. The GLC did have a policy of offering building workers transfers to other sites, but because the area that the council covered was so vast, they offered the most militant workers transfers to sites in less accessible places furthest away in West London in the hope that they wouldn't take up the offers. One of those carpenters, a Welshman called Ronnie Rees (known on site as 'Red Ron'), told everyone that a company called *M. J. Gleeson Ltd.* was taking on carpenters at the construction of a multi-million pound contract to build a new power station at Dartford in Kent just the other side of the Dartford tunnel.

He said that he was going to the site, Littlebrook 'D' Power Station, the following day to fill in an application form. Eight of us decided to go with him. When I filled in the form, I didn't put down my National Insurance number. Most of the others didn't do either, mostly because they couldn't remember them. I knew

One of the wooden vestibules on the front of the flats in Briar Road that Peter and I built.

Littlebrook 'D' Power Station site

mine only too well, but I didn't put it on the form because I knew that it was a way that employers could identify trade union activists. Many militants had changed their names to avoid being refused work on sites, but one thing that can't be changed is a person's National Insurance number. The other eight lads all got an immediate start whilst I was sent a letter saying that I would be considered for employment once I had provided my National Insurance number. I provided my National Insurance number, but I heard nothing back from them. This was despite the fact that I was one of only two of the nine applicants who had an Advanced City and Guilds certificate in carpentry and joinery. I decided to soldier on at the GLC site for a while.

Chapter 4

Thrown into the lions' den!

Three months had passed since I applied for a job on the Littlebrook 'D' Power Station site with *M. J. Gleeson Ltd.* and I had heard nothing from them. I was convinced that this was because of my trade union activity, especially on the GLC site at Harold Hill. Then, out of the blue, I suddenly received a letter from *M. J. Gleeson Ltd.* asking me to come for an interview. I attended the interview which was with one of the site agents called Andy (there were several site agents as it was a very large site) who said, after he'd interviewed me 'I can't believe that we haven't sent for you earlier'. I just shrugged my shoulders and said that I didn't know why either. Anyway, I was given the job and said that I'd start the following Monday.

The following Monday I started on the site and was assigned by Andy to the joinery workshop foreman Steve, working in the workshop and in the yard on the site making up formwork, or 'shutters' as they are colloquially called. Whilst Steve was standing explaining to me what he wanted me to do, I saw Roy Wales, a guy who I had worked with on the GLC site, coming up behind him with his index finger to his lips. He obviously didn't want me to indicate in front of Steve that I knew him. All three of us chatted for a couple of minutes until Steve left me to get on with it. Once Steve had gone, Roy said to me 'I bet you're surprised to be here Jack?' With a wry smile on my face, I nodded in agreement.

Roy explained that he had been made up to a foreman on the site and had subsequently said to Andy, the site agent, that he needed more chippies. Andy had said to him that the site industrial relations officer was on holiday, so could Roy go into his office and get the file of completed application forms out of his filing cabinet and suggest suitable candidates. Roy went on to explain that when he did this, he found that there were two files of application forms in the filing cabinet, one of which had written on the front 'Not to be employed under any circumstances'. He decided to look in this file and when he did, he discovered that my application form was on top of the pile. He took it out and put it on top of the completed forms in the other file. He then took the file to Andy and said that I looked like a good candidate. Andy agreed and that's why he had called me for an interview. No wonder he was surprised that I hadn't been called for an interview before!

This was clear evidence that blacklisting was going on, but I couldn't say anything because I would have dropped Roy right in it and, after all, he had done me a great favour. The site industrial relations officer was Bill Kelly, a UCATT member himself and Branch Secretary of the Deptford branch of the union. He was clearly collaborating with the employers to blacklist certain workers. I was later told by sympathetic office staff that when he returned from holiday and found out that I'd been taken on that he was furious. He knew my dad from UCATT functions that they had both attended and platforms that they had shared and he clearly knew me as well. However, I worked in that yard next to the offices for weeks making up shutters and he passed me nearly every day going to his office. He always looked the other way as he passed and never acknowledged that he knew who I was, until one day after six weeks when he suddenly said 'Hello Jack. How's your dad?' I just said 'OK'.

The client was the *Central Electricity Generating Board* (CEGB) and there was about a dozen major contractors on site, including a steel erecting firm, boilermakers, a tunnel mining company, catering and electrical contractors as well as numerous sub-contracting firms. The building company *John Laing* had been the main construction company on site for some time and they had expected to get the contract for the second phase of building work. My branch secretary, Ted Childs, was working as a carpenter for *Laing's*, as was CPGB member Dave Hardie who I was later to have many dealings with because he was elected as a UCATT full-time official and then promoted to Eastern Regional Secretary.

Despite *Laing's* expectations, *M. J. Gleeson Ltd.* had put in a successful bid of £17 million for the second phase of work; not an inconsiderable sum in the 1970s. A power station is a huge civil engineering undertaking and usually takes about 10 years to complete. *M. J.*

Gleeson Ltd were not known for undertaking such large ventures and were more known as a middle-sized housebuilding company. As such they were not used to dealing with trade unions on such large projects and this was later to become fairly evident. It's probably the reason why they employed a right-wing trade unionist in Bill Kelly as a site industrial relations officer.

Anyway, I had only been there a couple of weeks when the company sacked Terry, a scaffolder, for a very minor misdemeanour on the Friday of his first week. Terry was a longstanding TGWU member. Remember, as I said before, the National Working Rule Agreement allowed companies to sack workers in the first week of employment for no reason. Nevertheless, suspecting that Terry had been sacked for a spurious reason, all the scaffolders walked off the site and sat in the canteen, followed by all the other workers.

The TGWU full-time official, Frank Byrne, was called in to negotiate with the firm. I got to know Frank fairly well over the next four years. He was a Labour Party member, an efficient full-time official and could be militant at times. After some lengthy negotiation with the director in charge of the site, he came back to a mass meeting in the canteen to explain that the company had not followed the proper procedure. The company, therefore, had agreed to let Terry serve his first week's probation once again and if he 'kept his nose clean' for the week, his job would be secure. Frank recommended accepting this compromise. There were a few workers who objected to this and said, 'why should he have to do his probationary week all over again, especially as the company had not followed the proper procedure?'. The majority, however, accepted my suggestion that such an olive branch to the company, who knew they were in the wrong, may be something that we need reciprocating in the future, especially as Frank added that he didn't think the company would dare to sack Terry during the following week on such spurious grounds again. They didn't!

After a few weeks making up shutters in the yard I, along with about a couple of dozen other chippies and labourers, was sent to work on constructing a 'tank farm' or pump station about a mile from the main site. We had to be transported there each morning in a company *Transit* van and brought back to the main site each evening to get cleaned up and clock out. As it was so far from the main site, it was suggested that we needed a shop steward to represent us. A meeting was called and Roy Wales, the foreman I mentioned earlier, suggested me. His nomination was seconded, but before a vote could take place I thought it was important that I explained that I was a member of the Communist Party and would take a militant stance on most issues. Everyone said that this was not a problem and in fact, many of them welcomed this. I was duly elected.

The shop stewards met infrequently in the trade union office which was on the corner of the temporary building housing the canteen and the changing rooms. Patsy was the convenor steward. Patsy had worked for the company for a number of years and, although a decent bloke, he had been brought to the site by the company in the expectation that he would become the convenor. A number of companies at the time used to attempt to 'install' shop stewards who were loyal company men in order to avoid any challenge to their authority. I wouldn't say that Patsy was a 'patsy' or 'company man' exactly but, although my experience was limited, he had even more limited experience of working for any other building contractors than me and he tended to accept things as they were.

At a meeting of all the shop stewards somebody proposed that I should take over as the convenor. Patsy was quite happy to stand down and I was seconded and duly elected. As the new convenor, I received, totally unsolicited, a CABIN 'action kit' putting the employers' case against nationalisation of the building industry. Despite the fact that my name was incorrectly spelt as 'Foubert', I wrote to CABIN saying that the 300 workers on the site in UCATT and the TGWU would be interested in hearing it justify its claims. An exchange of letters followed in which a CABIN employee and former Deputy Project Manager at the Littlebrook site, J.A. Armitt, produced figures that 70 per cent of those in the industry opposed nationalisation. In a site meeting called to ostensibly discuss other matters, the overwhelming majority of my members said that they didn't even know what the Labour Party's proposals for construction were!

So, in a bid to enlighten them, on December 11th the works committee wrote to CABIN inviting them to the site to debate the issue in a site meeting in the canteen. It was not until January 23rd that we received a letter from CABIN director Tony Smith, refusing a debate. The letter said: 'We feel that a mass meeting on the site is not an appropriate forum.' In the letter, he went on to offer us supplies of CABIN material for distribution on site. The drubbing they received at the debate the previous November at Conway Hall had obviously made them reluctant to face workers' representatives again. It seemed that they preferred to stick to expensive poster campaigns, flying hot air balloons at TUC conferences and showing anti-nationalisation films on site with no right of reply to putting its case in a debate.

It wasn't long, however, before I had to deal with a major dispute and I have to say that neither I nor the works committee in general were ready for it. The scaffolding shop steward, Billy Walsh, was sacked for refusing an order from Andy, the site agent who had taken me on. It was usual at the time on large civil engineering projects, that were by their very nature risky places to work, for scaffolders to work in pairs. Andy had sent Billy to an isolated area of the site to erect scaffolding on his own. As soon as I heard about the sacking, I went to see Andy and the industrial relations officer, Bill Kelly, to ask that we discuss this and see if we could come to some sort of agreement. Andy was having none of it and was adamant that Billy was sacked and that was the end of the matter.

I had no alternative but to call a mass meeting in the canteen, at which the workforce voted to strike. There was only one long road of about a mile into the site from the Dartford tunnel where we set up a picket line. Historically, large civil engineering projects like power station construction had been marked by almost perpetual industrial unrest, not least because with so many contractors, when the workers with one contractor walked out, they would picket the site and trade unionists with other companies would always refuse to cross the picket line. Indeed, I was brought up to believe, and still do believe, as did most trade unionists at the time, that you should NEVER cross a picket line. This meant that such projects were almost continually dogged by complete shutdowns because one group of workers or another was invariably on strike.

In an attempt to avert these problems and with the support of the client, the CEGB, Danny O'Connor, the convenor steward with *John Laing*, had set up a 'Liaison Committee' of convenors and shop stewards from all the major contractors to meet regularly to try to help to resolve such disputes. The agreement between them was that when one company's workers went on strike and were on the picket line, they would not stop workers from other companies crossing that line. In return, the Liaison Committee would do everything it could to put pressure on the CEGB and the contractor concerned to resolve the dispute.

So, we allowed other contractors' workers to cross the picket line. In hindsight, this was a mistake as the Liaison Committee did little to help resolve the dispute. If we had stopped the whole site then it is more likely that pressure would have been brought to bear on *M.*

J. Gleeson by both the client, the CEGB, and the other contractors to negotiate a settlement. Indeed, many of the workers with other contractors told us that they felt uncomfortable about crossing a picket line and that we should stop everyone. Even some of the works committee on *Laing's* didn't agree with their own convenor steward about this.

One *Laing's* worker in particular, the scaffolder shop steward, 'Tarmac Billy' as he was known, was very vociferous in saying that we should ignore the Liaison Committee. He was a CPGB member and was called 'Tarmac Billy' because every time he had a disagreement with management, he would say 'let's hit the tarmac', meaning to go outside on the road and picket the site. We did have mass pickets and stop everyone on a few occasions just to remind them that we were still there, but it should have been every day.

During the dispute, we had a number of meetings with management to try to find a resolution, but they played hardball every time. As the convenor steward, I had to deal with a number of people in management on a day-to-day basis. Although foremen were all trade union members as part of the closed shop, some were more committed 'company men' rather than 'union men'. I got to find out, for example, that Steve, the foreman I had been put with on my first day, could be a bit of a blabbermouth to management. That's why Roy Wales had acted in the way that he had when he first met me on site. There were also four or five site agents. The most difficult to deal with was Bill Longhurst. Bill had the attitude that we should all just be grateful that the company had given us jobs rather than the company being grateful that the workers were making huge profits for them.

Most of my dealings as convenor steward, however, were with the site industrial relations officer, Bill Kelly. Whilst I had a great deal of contempt for him, not just because of how he'd tried to keep me off the site but also because of his devious betrayal of trade union principles, I was pleasant enough to him most of the time because of the amount of time that we were forced to spend together. On the other hand, although in a more senior position, John Sheehan, the Construction Manager, was someone who I got on well with. We had our differences and sometimes we had stand-up rows, but John was a pragmatic man who wore his heart on his sleeve, always upfront with me and didn't have a devious bone in his body. In breaks in negotiations and at other times he also liked discussing Irish political history with me and wanted to know what my thoughts were on the Irish struggles and Irish political leaders; James Connolly, Michael Collins and Eamon De Valera in particular.

When major, rather than day-to-day, issues needed to be discussed, as was the case in this dispute, I would meet with the Project Manager and company director, Ian Lamont, or his deputy Brian. They were like chalk and cheese. Ian Lamont was a hard-headed Scot who was a tough negotiator. He would often have his 'financial advisor', Barry, with him. Barry was a highly educated man and Ian Lamont relied on him for advice, especially when it came to discussing the company bonus scheme; more about that later. I would always try to take at least one other shop steward in with me when meeting Ian Lamont, so that I could never be accused of doing deals behind others' backs.

Brian, the Deputy Project Manager, on the other hand, was very different. He seemed to hold the position of Deputy Project Manager because of his experience and qualifications as a civil engineer. He was a quiet man who didn't like conflict with trade unions and clearly seemed embarrassed at having to deal with shop stewards.

Back to the dispute. Whenever we, the shop stewards, went into the site for negotiations with the management, Bill Kelly was always there. As I said, there was only one road into the site that we knew of and nobody on the picket line ever saw him cross it. As a trade unionist, he shouldn't cross picket lines anyway and some of the pickets relished the idea of giving him some stick if he did cross. I later learnt from a reliable source in the offices that he was always smuggled in to the site in the boot of a manager's car when negotiations were due to take place. What a weasel!

The strike dragged on for four weeks. One of the carpenters who worked in the workshop on site, Don, was a traveller and he had a truck. Anything we wanted, such as tarpaulins to keep us dry, a brazier to keep us warm and so on, he would go off and 'scrounge' from somewhere for us. We had a good picket rota going and for the whole time we never had any shortage of volunteers to staff the picket line.

During that time, we had several visitors to the picket line. On one occasion a group of young students who were all members of the Socialist Workers' Party (SWP) came to the picket line and started telling the pickets what they ought to be doing. One older steel fixer said to me 'who the f**k are these people Jack? Why don't you just tell them to f**k off?' I told him that it would be better coming from him because if I told them, they'd probably call me a 'typical union bureaucrat' or something like that because I was an official of the union. So, the steel fixer told them in no uncertain terms that he'd worked in the building industry all his life and he wasn't going to be told what he should or shouldn't be doing during a strike by 'wet behind the ears students'. They soon disappeared. In contrast, we had members of the local Trades Council and the local Labour Party visit the picket line and they just simply asked us how they could help; the correct way for supporters of a strike to behave and we were all grateful for their support.

After four weeks, although nobody had tried to break the strike, cracks were beginning to appear. The strike was unofficial, as most disputes on big sites were in those days, for two reasons. Firstly, the unions, UCATT in particular, didn't have the funds to support every stoppage on every site and secondly, although there were left-wingers in the UCATT leadership, most full-time officials of the union were fairly right-wing. So, we never got any strike pay. That meant that all of us had to go off and find other cash-in-hand work that we could do on days that we weren't assigned to picket duty. As convenor steward, I had to be on the picket line most days, so, although I got some 'private carpentry jobs', I had to do them mostly at weekends. My childhood friend, Ray, who I'd worked with at *Durable Suites* and *Quinn's*, had also got a job on the site and together we made a set of hardwood window frames for the whole house of a neighbour of his in my garage. This was in the days before uPVC window frames became popular. Nevertheless, this was all starting to get very stressful for everyone.

What didn't help was the sacked scaffolder, Billy Walsh's bombastic, rather than humble, attitude towards the 300 workers that had come out on strike in support of him. There were also an increasing number of rumours circulating, ones that I was continually having to quash, that as an Irish Protestant, he didn't really care about the Irish Catholic workers on site and didn't really represent them. Others were saying that after four weeks, we had tried our best to get him reinstated, but that we were now fighting a losing battle. The works committee called a meeting and there was a majority vote to return to work rather than see a gradual drift back. We apologised to Billy that we had done all that we could but that we had to accept defeat on this occasion.

Back on site, there was so much that needed to be addressed that we argued that, like the convenor stewards on all the other companies on site, I needed to be made full-time. There were some *Gleeson* workers on site who opposed this, saying that I should be out on site, having to do what everyone else had to do; that is having to graft really hard on heavy and difficult work in all kinds of weather conditions, rather than, in their words, 'sitting and drinking cups of tea with management all day'. Several others who had experience of working on large projects elsewhere, convinced the doubters that they'd rather see me in the offices fighting for better wages and conditions than out on site. Roy Wales, being in the position of foreman and able to move around the site talking to workers, was the most effective ally that I had in this regard.

The company and the Project Director, Ian Lamont, in particular, initially opposed having a full-time convenor of shop stewards as well, but, given that it was an almost universal practice on site amongst other contractors and the fact that there were so many things that needed sorting out, he reluctantly relented. I suspect that the client, the CEGB, may have had a quiet word about it to him as well.

The first thing that I needed to do was to build an effective organisation. I managed to get agreement from the company for a works committee of one main shop steward from each trade to meet once a week in the union office. In addition, the company agreed to recognise other shop stewards from different areas of the site to feed information through their main representative on the works committee informally and in a meeting of all shop stewards in the canteen once a month. Eventually, we had a works committee of seven shop stewards, including myself as convenor.

Mick was the carpenters' main shop steward. He was a diminutive but tenacious character who was very meticulous in gathering and presenting evidence to management. Frank was the bricklayers' shop steward. He was from Southend-On-Sea, had been a solid trade unionist all his working life, a regular attender at his branch and had a very wry sense of humour, especially when dealing with the more obtuse members of management. Tommy was the scaffolders' new shop steward. He was related to Billy Walsh (I think they were cousins) and he was the youngest one amongst us. He was a bit naïve at times, but his heart was always in the right place.

Con was the labourers shop steward. He was a thoughtful man who loved his philosophy and had read everything from Plato to Marx. He could, however, on occasions be obstinate and show a lack of tact. I remember in particular on one occasion being with him in negotiations with Ian Lamont where we were getting close to the point of convincing the Project Manager of the legitimacy of our case when Con suddenly said to him, 'Of course, if you don't agree, then we'll be out of the gate!' That was like a red rag to a bull and Lamont simply replied: 'Oh well, if that's the case, then do your worst' and refused to discuss the issue any more. I was furious with Con. Brian was the shop steward for the yard where all the pre-cast units were made. He had been transferred to the site from a South London site by the company; but Brian was no 'company man'.

Johnny was the steel fixers' shop steward. He was a very intelligent and articulate worker who I understood had been an architect, but had given it up because he preferred to work 'with the lads' on site. He had previously worked for *John Laing* on the Littlebrook site and had been a shop steward there. Johnny was a committed socialist, a *Morning Star* reader and a militant. Like Pat Tracey at the GLC site, he was pretty close to the CPGB, but I think he wouldn't join because of the party's stance on abortion being at odds with his Catholicism. He was also one of the scruffiest people you would ever be likely to meet. He was known as 'tatty head' by many fellow workers because of his habit of putting a filthy knotted handkerchief on his head in the hot weather. In addition to the seven works committee members, by the time the contract reached its peak we had 20 other shop stewards on site, making a total of 27 who would meet once a month just before monthly mass meetings.

In 1977 Sue and I had our second child, another boy that we called Nicky. During that year, there were numerous activities in which I became involved, both on and off the site. For example, occasionally the TGWU full-time official, Frank Byrne, would contact me and ask if I could help by getting a few lads together to come and help out on a picket line somewhere else on his patch. He had to ring the office on site and they would come and get me. Despite nearly every other convenor of other contractors on site having a phone in their union office, *Gleeson's* would not agree to this, insisting that I could only use the phone in the construction manager, John Sheehan's, office. To be fair to John, he would always leave his office when I was on the phone.

Anyway, one such time Frank asked if I could bring some lads to a site in Dartford where a smallish employer was resisting demands for union recognition. About half the lads were out on a picket line, but about half were crossing the picket line and going to work. The pickets needed reinforcements and we obliged. We tried to persuade delivery drivers to not cross the picket line and to turn around at the entrance to the site. Most obliged, including Royal Mail drivers. One tipper lorry driver, however, just shouted 'f**k you and your unions' and drove straight at Frank who had to dive out of the way into the mud.

Now, Frank was usually a reasonable man, but when he lost his temper, he was a different kettle of fish. He got up, red in the face in a rage, and started hurling bricks, rocks and lumps of concrete at this lorry and we all joined in. The driver tipped his load of sand on the site as we were throwing everything we could into the box at the back. So, the driver kept the box up as he drove off the site, taking down the overhead telephone wires as he went. He had just turned the corner when a police car came round from the other direction and seeing wires all over the road, one of the officers said 'what the hell's been going on here?' As calm as you like, Frank introduced himself as the TGWU official and said 'I don't know officer. This madman just drove straight at all of us and then drove off with his box still up, bringing down the wires. I got his number if you'd like it.' The officer thanked Frank for this information and said that the driver would pay dearly for what he'd done.

On another occasion, Frank rang me to ask for help picketing a roadworks site in South London. The employer was the infamous *Murphy's* who was well-known for employing lump labour under terrible conditions. I rounded up several lads who wanted to go to help out. When we got there, the site was between two roundabouts. We reinforced the picket line and stopped all lorries from crossing. The local coppers didn't know what to do. Within no time at all, though, the Special Patrol Group (SPG) were there. The 'top brass' never came to see us or the trade union officials to discuss the dispute, but immediately went up the road where we could see them talking to John Murphy himself for about five minutes.

Then, a Black Maria was backed up to the picket line and the back doors were opened. The copper in charge with all the pips on his shoulders walked up to the picket line and, without asking any of the strikers or trade union officials any questions, said, 'Anyone not out of the road in two minutes will be thrown in the back of there and arrested for obstruction'. After a couple of minutes protesting, Frank thanked us all for our support and advised us to get out of the road as we had made our point and he didn't want any of us to get arrested for simply supporting his members. It was a further demonstration to me of the class bias of policing industrial disputes in Britain.

A stark reminder of this also came in that summer at the *Grunwick Film Processing Laboratories* in Willesden in North London where a strike had started the previous year. The strikers were mostly female, immigrant, East African Asians, dubbed by the media as 'strikers in saris'. They were led by the diminutive but redoubtable Jayaben Desai. The average pay of the workers was £28 per week while the average national wage was £72 per week and the average full-time wage for a female manual worker in London was £44 per week. Overtime was compulsory and often no prior notice would be given that workers had overtime to do. Petty restrictions were imposed on workers, there was a bullying attitude on the part of supervision and frequent dismissals and threats of dismissals took place. In fact, the wages and conditions were described by one Labour MP as 'deplorable'. Remember that there was no National Minimum Wage at that time. It was the first time that such exploited immigrant labour had been supported in such numbers by the overwhelming majority of British trade unionists.

Indeed, it became a *cause celebre* for trade unionists and at its height involved thousands of trade unionists and police in confrontations, with over 500 arrests for picketing offences and frequent police violence, particularly by the SPG, against pickets. Because the company, led by George Ward and supported by Tory anti-union front organisations, were bussing in scabs to undermine the strike, a mass picket was called for 22nd June, 1977. We had a mass meeting on our site and decided to strike for the day and for as many of us as possible to go to support the mass picket. Workers came from all over Britain to support the strikers. Yorkshire miners' leader, Arthur Scargill, brought 5,000 Yorkshire miners to London and they marched from the station to the picket line. Along the way, journalists kept asking him what he and his men intended to do. His answer was always the same: 'Whatever the strike committee want us to do. It is their strike, not ours.'

There were a number of mass pickets in June and July which I attended along with other workers from the Littlebrook site. I witnessed the police violence at first hand and the way that the Asian women were continually intimidated. The company refused to meet with the workers' trade union, *The Association of Professional, Executive, Clerical and Computer Staff* (APEX), or the *Advisory, Conciliation and Arbitration Service* (ACAS) to discuss the dispute, preferring to offer to reinstate the workers on better pay and conditions if they agreed to give up their trade union membership. The workers voted against this.

The Labour government decided to commission an inquiry under Lord Scarman and the pickets were called off to wait for the result of the inquiry. APEX announced that it would abide by the outcome of the inquiry but Ward did not, saying he would only submit to the normal courts. The enquiry recommended both trade union recognition and re-instatement of the workers, but Ward, backed by the right-wing *National Association for Freedom* (NAFF) and the Tories, rejected the recommendations. The TUC subsequently and disgracefully withdrew their support. Even more disgracefully, Jayaben Desai was suspended from APEX in November 1977 following her hunger strike outside TUC headquarters. The workers' strike committee announced the end of the dispute in June 1978. To this day, Jayaben Desai remains one of my all-time heroes. What a woman!

Back on the Littlebrook site, the biggest bone of contention was the bonus scheme. It's worth explaining some background to incentive schemes in the construction industry in general before talking more about parochial issues. Until 1947 payment-by-results schemes were forbidden by all the craft unions who believed that adherence to the 'plain-time rate' and everyone fighting to improve that together, strengthened their organisations. Also, in an industry where unemployment between jobs was endemic, it was argued that any incentive schemes would just see members working themselves out of jobs even faster.

However, after the second world war there was a mass housebuilding programme launched to clear the 19th century slums and to repair the damage done by six years of war (Why can't they do that today?). There was pressure on the unions to accept incentive schemes, especially as it was the first majority Labour government that was trying to transform Britain for the benefit of the whole working-class. A deal was done to introduce payment-by-results schemes on an individual site or company basis. The plumbing and electrical trade unions refused to enter such an agreement. It was left up to each company to introduce their own individual schemes or to pay a fixed minimum bonus if they chose not to.

What this meant was that on the larger, organised sites, shop stewards were able to challenge their particular site or company's scheme or individual targets and so increase wages further than on unorganised sites by militant action. This meant that over the next three decades, shop stewards became more important in determining the wages of workers than full-time officials, especially as a gradual 'wage drift' made the 'plain-time rate' increasingly irrelevant. It failed to keep up with the 'plain-time rates' of electricians and plumbers, let alone with basic pay in other industries. By the 1970s, on some of the major sites in London and other big cities, convenors and shop stewards had been able to negotiate bonuses that often trebled the wages of workers on site. This was the environment that I was thrown into. Many of the newer workers on *Gleeson's* had, indeed, worked on big sites before where the shop stewards had managed to negotiate very lucrative incentive payments.

By 1976 the basic weekly pay for craftsmen had risen to £37.00 per week and £31.40 for labourers. The guaranteed minimum weekly bonus (GMB) was £11.00 (27.5p an hour) for craftsmen and £10.20 for labourers with a £4 cost of living supplement for craftsmen and a £3.60 cost of living supplement for labourers added in June 1977 (Wood, 1979: 198). The latter was as a consequence of the wage restraint brought in by the Labour government's so-called 'social contract' with the trade unions (I, like many others, referred to it as the 'social con-trick'). Most other contractors on site had bonus schemes that were based on individual trades. The *Gleeson* bonus scheme, however, paid exactly the same bonus to every worker, whether bricklayer or carpenter and whether skilled or unskilled. The argument from the company was that a premium for skilled workers was reflected in basic rates of pay and the bonus should be the same for everyone for their collective effort; a view that, incidentally, I agreed with, not least because it gave workers a common sense of purpose on site.

There were some workers on site, however, that thought that this was unfair, frequently citing the labourer whose job it was to clean the toilets and keep the changing rooms tidy. Compared to what most workers had to do out on site, it was a fairly easy, unskilled job. What didn't help was the cleaner's constant bleating about how hard his job was, despite my attempts to tell him to cool it. This really wound up many of those who worked out on the site. Nevertheless, overall, most agreed with the principle that everyone should get the same. Whilst *Gleeson's* bonus scheme was averaging around 60p an hour (£24.00 a week), other building workers with other companies on the Littlebrook site and with contractors on other large sites in the big cities, £2.00 an hour or £80 a week was more like the benchmark.

The works committee started putting pressure on the company to explain why the bonus payments were so 'low' in comparison to other big civil engineering contracts and to what was being paid by other contractors on site. The way that the bonus scheme worked was (deliberately?) presented to us in such a complicated way, that it was difficult for us to get to the bottom of it. We had meeting after meeting with the management, but could get nowhere. So, we decided to recommend industrial action, but this time we had learnt a lesson that all-out strike action was not the best way to approach the problem. So, over several months, we embarked on a series of disruptive stoppages. We tried each trade stopping for one day at a time, everybody striking for days when vital work needed completing, 'go slows' and so on.

Nevertheless, some of the non-works committee shop stewards thought that I and the works committee were not doing enough and were ineffective in our battles with the company over the bonus payments. They met clandestinely without the knowledge of the works committee and voted to take action independently. The most vociferous of the 'gang of twenty' was a steel fixer shop steward called Geoff. When I found out, I was furious and called a meeting of all the shop stewards and announced that my position as convenor steward had become untenable. I resigned, continuing as a shop steward for the carpenters, and the meeting elected Geoff as Convenor steward.

Chapter 5

Here we go again!

I went back to working on the tools in the workshop and yard. It was only a matter of days before the foreman Roy Wales approached me and warned me to be careful as he had overheard talk between the site agents in the office of plans 'to get me' because they saw me as being in a weakened position. It wasn't long before one site agent, the aforementioned Bill Longhurst, had me up in front of Bill Kelly, the site industrial relations officer, for a verbal warning for a minor misdemeanour; one which would have been overlooked if it had been committed by anyone else. He had caught me making a very small personal item that took no more than a few minutes during working time.

Later on, I was then transferred to a remote part of the site where it would have been difficult, if not impossible, to represent the carpenters. Spontaneously, and without any complaint or prompt from me, all 80 carpenters walked off the main site and sat in the canteen. Ian Lamont came to see me and asked me if I'd go into the canteen and persuade them to go back to work. My reply was 'You've created this situation. You solve it. I'm not Henry Kissinger, your special envoy!' Bill Longhurst was sent into the canteen to ask them to go back to work, but he was sent away with a flea in his ear with the reply supported by all the carpenters of 'Yes we will, when you stop picking on Jack Fawbert!' The company, realising that I had the overwhelming support of the carpenters, sent me back to work in the workshop and yard and the carpenters all went back to work. This put me in a much stronger position, knowing that the carpenters had my back. I owed them.

Over the next couple of months it became obvious that, although I was relatively inexperienced as an active trade unionist, Geoff was totally out of his depth. He would frequently make poor decisions, get nowhere with his belligerent attitude in negotiations with management and drop clangers in mass meetings with the workers on site. He would also often come to me for advice about what he should do about various issues. Although I was still aggrieved about the uncomradely way that he had acted that had forced me to resign as convenor steward, I always gave him the best advice that I could, because to do otherwise would have been to the detriment of my fellow workers; something that I would never contemplate.

Nevertheless, Geoff eventually realised that his bravado was not matched by his ability to deliver for the workers on site and he resigned. A meeting of all 27 shop stewards was called and I was asked by them, including all the 'rebels', if I would take over as convenor again. My reply was that I would only do so on the understanding that in future we make collective decisions that are binding on all of us and that we work together for the common good; no more mavericks meeting clandestinely in other words. This was agreed and I became the convenor steward again.

From my first stint as convenor steward I had learnt some valuable lessons. Whilst the all-out strike over the sacking of Billy Walsh had been necessary, all-out strike action wasn't always the best option. Sometimes it certainly was necessary, but sometimes selective action was a better option, sometimes legal routes could be used (though they should never be relied upon) and sometimes the industry machinery was the best route to take. I adopted the old adage of 'horses for courses'!

Also, I had to be craftier in building up networks to get as much information as I could about what the management were up to before recommending courses of action to the works committee. Bearing in mind that this was pre-computer days and all documents were paper ones, all the office waste material was dumped in the skip outside the workshop. Don, the traveller I mentioned earlier, was promoted to foreman of the workshop in the yard when Steve left. Don would rummage through the skip to see if there was anything that might be useful to me, which from time to time there was. Also, I got to know one or two of the office staff well enough, including the project manager's personal secretary, that they would feed me tit-bits of useful information.

In terms of site conditions, these were mostly in line with or better than the minimum required by the National Working Rule Agreement. This was on the insistence of the client, the CEGB. There were proper toilet facilities housed in large portacabins, there were changing rooms and a canteen that served tea and coffee. If anyone wanted a hot meal, they could go to the canteen that was provided by the CEGB and staffed by a private contractor that was available for the workers of all contractors on site. The company provided luxury coaches to bring workers from South London and the Southend-On-Sea area to the site. Those coming from other parts of Essex and the South East had to find their own way to the site.

So, I needed to sort out the travelling expenses for those workers coming from the Essex side of the Dartford Tunnel each day that were not provided with transport. The National Agreement for Civil Engineering projects that we were working under stated that:

Travel expenses should be calculated as the crow flies from the worker's home to the site, except where there is a major river or mountain range. In the case of a major river or mountain range, the calculation should be made as the crow flies to the nearest crossing point, across that crossing point and then as the crow flies to the site [or words to that effect].

The company was, understandably, using the Dartford Tunnel as the nearest crossing point. However, the Dartford Tunnel was the first river crossing point in the UK for which there was a toll. Initially, it was 25p each way; a burden that we as workers were bearing. However, in December, 1977 this was increased to 35p each way or £3.50 per week. I argued that the company should either pay workers this fee or they should calculate travelling expenses to the nearest FREE crossing point, which would have been the Woolwich Ferry; much further upstream. This was a moot point in the national agreement, but the company would do neither.

So, I decided to use the industry machinery and referred the case to the Civil Engineering Industrial Tribunal. I prepared the case very carefully and at the tribunal held in Central London, I presented it to a committee of some of the leading industrialists in building and civil engineering. *Gleeson's* chief industrial relations officer was there putting the case for the company. In response to the case that I had put forward, Kenneth McAlpine said to me that if we all got paid the tolls, we could come four in a car to work and actually make money out of it. I responded by saying that we weren't trying to make money out of it, but just wanted compensating for our losses and that if three workers had to meet up with a driver somewhere on the Essex side of the river, they would collectively be travelling further anyway. The judgement was that 'no worker should be left out of pocket by having to pay the toll fees', or words to that effect.

When we returned to site, we met with the company's chief industrial relations officer to hammer out a deal. His immediate offer was that they would pay a quarter of the fees incurred by each worker as they could travel four in a car. He wouldn't budge from this. So, I said that there was no point in continuing to discuss it and led my fellow shop stewards out of the meeting, saying as a parting shot that 'we'll just have to go back to the tribunal then!'

Within half-an-hour we were called back into the office and a compromise was suggested that they pay half on the assumption that, on average, two workers travelled in each car. We accepted this on the understanding that the payments would be backdated to when workers from the North side of the Thames had started on the site. We knew that if we went back to the tribunal, they would almost certainly rule that any agreement should be retrospective. So, they agreed to this. One pound seventy-five pence a week was quite a considerable sum in those days and, with it being made retrospective, many workers on the site were delighted and expressed their appreciation for what we'd achieved when they got their wage packets the following week. Whilst it didn't benefit all the workers on site and it was only a minor victory, I think that it gave everyone a lift and the confidence to think that the company were not invincible when it came to battles with us.

Personally, I did actually benefit from this arrangement as I usually travelled to work with Tony and Dave, two really good lads who I'd worked with at the GLC site, and Terry, a steel fixer foreman who lived in my street. So, each of us only had to use our cars once every four weeks. Other workers came singly or in pairs. So, on average the assumption of two workers in each car was just about right. As we've seen with regard to people like Mick Lynch recently, those who represent workers are often falsely accused, especially by the mainstream media, of doing so in order to benefit themselves.

Being convenor steward, during my four years on the site this was the only way in which I benefitted more than some other workers. Being a full-time convenor, I didn't get extra payments for unsocial hours, using specialist equipment or working in dirty conditions, for example, and I got the same bonus as everyone else. I was also often out of pocket for travelling around outside of working hours for the benefit of my members. Also, on unforeseen occasions, I would be locked in negotiations with management way beyond clocking-out time. I didn't get any overtime payments for this, not that I would have wanted any, but more importantly, I had to leave Tony, Dave and Terry waiting for me in the car park to go home.

On occasion, I had to tell Ian Lamont that they were waiting for me in the car park when negotiations unexpectedly went on past finishing time. He said to let them go and he would take me home, but I never accepted his offer and never would as a matter of principle. When I knew that I would be in negotiations with management that were likely to go on beyond the normal finishing time I would come to work in my own car. On one occasion, when I'd come to work in one of the other lads' cars, I clocked out and travelled by train up to the TGWU offices in Tooley Street in London to attend a hastily organised meeting with Peter Kavanagh, the TGWU Regional Secretary and Ian Lamont, the Project Manager of *Gleeson's*. The meeting went on until the early evening. At the conclusion of the meeting, Ian Lamont offered me a lift home as he was going past where I lived on his way home to the Southend area. I refused as usual, even though I had to get several trains to get back to Aveley late at night.

It was very easy to get sucked into having cosy relationships with employers and their representatives. Some trade union officials were known for having 'business meetings' with employers over lunch or over a game of golf that the employers paid for, but I was always extremely careful to separate business and pleasure. The most I ever accepted from *Gleeson's*, or from any other employer for that matter, was a cup of tea or a fag during negotiations (at that time everyone used to pass their fags round the table at negotiations).

Well, that's not strictly true. During that time, I was building a kitchen extension on my house at Aveley. High quality and high-density insulation blocks were being used by the bricklayers on the Littlebrook site. I noticed that any that had even the smallest chip out of the corner of them were thrown into the skip. I asked the Construction Manager, John Sheehan, what would happen to them and he said that they would just be thrown away. I asked if, therefore, I could take some of them as the chips didn't matter as my extension was to be pebble dashed. He said 'Of course and you can borrow one of the company vans to take them away at the weekend if you like.'

I first declined his offer of the use of a company van, until he said that this wasn't a privilege that he was giving especially to me; that other workers on the site had been allowed to use the company vans at weekends as long as they brought them back with the same amount of petrol in them as when they had borrowed them. I therefore accepted his offer, but I made sure that everyone on site knew about the arrangement. I just thought that it's important to put the record straight, not just for myself but also for all those other active trade unionists who sacrifice their own incomes and welfare in order to represent their fellow workers.

Back to the 'bonus battles'. We continued with a campaign to fight for higher bonus payments. On some occasions when we did go on strike, we had visits to the picket line from various journalists and on one occasion in particular, none other than the right-wing *Daily Express* journalist, Chapman Pincher came asking questions. Pincher was a well-known anti-communist who saw 'Soviet spies' everywhere and 'reds under the bed' infiltrating British institutions. A few of the lads recognised him and decided to have a bit of fun at his expense, not letting on that they knew who he was. Pincher asked them that if they weren't getting any strike pay, how did they manage? They replied that the Soviet Union was helping them through the Communist Party and he actually put in his column in the *Daily Express* that he'd been told this by reliable sources! No wonder that the great socialist historian, E.P. Thompson wrote that 'Mr. Pincher is too self-important and light-witted to realize how often he is being used' (Fowler, 2021).

On one occasion when we went on strike and stopped everyone from crossing the picket line, the queue was building up to get on the site, when the local copper arrived on his bike. He asked who was in charge and I said that I was. He said:

Look, if this carries on and the queue gets any longer it will tail back to and block the Dartford Tunnel. In no time at all you'll have the SPG (Special Patrol Group) down here and there'll be serious aggro. I don't want that any more than you do. I just want a quiet life. Here's my suggestion. I set up a roundabout where the lay-by is and direct all the traffic around it, but if someone insists on going into the site, I'll have to let them, but I'll make sure that you have a chance to speak to them first, okay? (Or words to that effect).

I said 'okay' and all the traffic was turning around until a bloke in a suit, puffing away on a big cigar turned up in his *Jaguar* (he looked just like a stereotypical boss). He opened the driver's door and shouted to the copper, and this is no word of a lie, 'get this riff-raff out of my way. I want to go into work.' One of our pickets approached him, put his hand on the door frame of his car and attempted to speak to him. He slammed the car door on the picket's arm. Immediately, our friendly neighbourhood copper rushed over and told the driver to turn around and go or he would arrest him for assault. He didn't argue and left. We never had any further trouble that day. That's often the difference with a local bobby.

On another occasion when we had a mass picket though, the police came in force and the senior officer in charge told me that I couldn't have more than six pickets. I reminded him that this was not the law but was only Home Office advice, as indeed it was at that time. This seemed to annoy him that I obviously knew the law more than he did and he told me that if everyone apart from six pickets didn't disperse, he would start ordering arrests to take place for public order offences. As I said, the road into the site was about a mile long. So, we set up picket lines of six pickets every few hundred yards along that road stopping traffic at all of them, telling the police that we were all in different disputes. This just made the queues longer. As soon as the police broke up one line, another one would appear further up the road. In the end they gave up.

One time when we were on strike, the London Regional Secretary of UCATT, Len Eaton, contacted me to ask us to withdraw the picket line on a particular day because he had a delegation of Soviet trade unionists coming to visit the site and it would be embarrassing if they were seen crossing a picket line. Now, Len was a right-winger who was one of the trade union leaders that had supported the *Cameron Report* (1967) recommendations that trade union leaders should ignore democratic site processes and support the sacking of militant shop stewards led by Lou Lewis on the Barbican site in the 1960s.

Although site reps were elected by the membership on site, shop steward and convenor steward credentials were issued by Regional Secretaries; and in theory could be withdrawn by Regional Secretaries, although this rarely happened because it would be seen by the rank-and-file as undermining democratic processes. Nevertheless, I was very wary of Len Eaton and didn't want to push my luck too far. Equally, we didn't want to embarrass Soviet trade unionists. So, we agreed, but I said that in return, he had to help us more than he had done previously in our dispute over the bonus scheme.

As London Regional Secretary, Len Eaton was the line manager of all the full-time elected officials in London and responsible for allocating areas for each of them to work in. He had allocated an official called Alf Alden to Dartford and the surrounding area because, as he and everyone else knew, Alf was not only right-wing but also, he was lazy and incompetent. Len had thought at the time that if he was kept out of the centre of London on the outskirts, he probably wouldn't have any large sites to deal with. Littlebrook 'D' was an aberration for the area. Alf had been elected at a time when there was nobody of a high enough calibre from the left, or the right come to that, to stand for election. As we will see later, he never kept up with developments in the industry or employment law and never went on any courses to improve his knowledge. So, that's why we asked Len to help.

Len and myself met with Ian Lamont and his 'financial advisor', Barry, at the site to try to reach some sort of agreement over the bonus payments. During lengthy negotiations it became clear that the bonus scheme was much less complicated than it had been presented to us previously. There was a straight linear relationship between production and bonus to be paid. The company said that this couldn't be changed as it was the basis on which the contract with the client, the CEGB, had been agreed. Len suggested that, as we had never earned over 60p an hour, perhaps an increasing or exponential returns line could be added to the graph over 60p and to tell the CEGB that the added line had always been there, but they hadn't known about it because we hadn't earnt that much before. This would be a great incentive, he argued, for the workers on site to increase their productivity, benefitting everyone in the bargain.

I was sceptical at first because this didn't increase our current bonus any more, but when we left the meeting, Len said to me: 'Now, you've got to get yourselves on that steeper curve by investigating more thoroughly how the bonus is worked out week by week and piece by piece. I thought: 'Well, we'll give it a go'. Bonuses were based on what the carpenters, bricklayers and steel fixers did each week. I got the stewards for those three trades together and said that what I wanted them to do was to keep detailed records of everything that their trades did on site, particularly 'extra' things that hadn't been planned for as well as recording every minute that our workers had been held up by work being done by other contractors because of a lack of coordination by the client, the CEGB. Each of them kept a little notebook where they noted everything down.

We then demanded to see the bonus sheets, as was our right, and to challenge them week by week in meetings with the respective site agents and the bonus clerk. I think we took the company a bit by surprise because they weren't expecting us to be so meticulous. I would go in with each steward in turn to discuss the bonus sheets with the relevant site agent and the bonus clerk. The bonus clerk was a guy called Fred who was just an employee who was there to record what we'd all done and work out the bonus. It was the site agent who, most of the time, we negotiated with. Fred was a pleasant bloke who I got on well with, not least because he was a supporter of West Ham United, like me. In any case, Fred rarely went out on site, sitting in his office most of the time just 'doing the sums' and so he couldn't challenge most of what we claimed anyway.

At first, we were astonished at the amount of time that hadn't been recorded that we were held up on site through no fault of our own and the amount of unplanned work that had been done that hadn't been recorded. Then we challenged them over particular targets which, on paper, seemed reasonable, but when explained why in practice they had taken so much longer meant that the company had no leg to stand on in setting such targets. Mick, the carpenter shop steward, was particularly good and tenacious in these negotiations. One fellow worker described him as 'like a little terrier dog who, once he'd got his teeth into something, wouldn't let go.'

In the end, every Thursday I would be in bonus negotiations all day, firstly with Mick, then with Frank, the bricklayers shop steward and then with Johnny, the steel fixer shop steward. Once we got onto that steeper curve, the hourly bonus started to rise rapidly to 80p, then up to £1.50, £2.00 and eventually after a year or more of wearing down the site agents and taking selective action, it settled at around £2.50 an hour each week. One week, it actually went up to £3.10! It was hard going at times, gradually wearing the management down, but I think we even surprised ourselves at how well we'd done in the end.

Whilst there were a few workers who moaned about all the stoppages, it was worth it in the end. A few years later I met a labourer called Dougie outside the Boleyn Ground at West Ham while queuing to go into a game. Dougie was a level-headed bloke who worked for *Gleeson's* for years, both before and after working on the Littlebrook 'D' site. He thanked me for all that I'd done and said that, despite all the industrial action, he'd never earned as much money in his life, either before or since the Littlebrook site. Because he was one of the first employees on the site and therefore one of the last to leave, he effectively had eight years there. I replied to him that 'it's not what I did Dougie, it's what we did together!'

There were numerous other issues that I had to deal with besides the bonus, though. On one occasion the lock-up for workers' tools was broken into and some tools were stolen. Under the National Working Rule Agreement, companies were obliged to provide secure lock-ups for tools and, as long as workers put their tools in the lock up, if any went missing, the company would be liable for up to £50 for each worker's loss. A carpenter called Colin Shilling made a claim on the company that all his tools had been stolen. It seemed a straightforward case until another carpenter, a Scot who was simply known as 'Jock', claimed that he too had all his tools stolen. I was sceptical about this and had him in my office and grilled him, telling him that if he was trying it on, he was just making it more difficult for Colin to get his compensation. He insisted that he wasn't trying it on.

The management were sceptical as well. Ian Lamont decided to ask 'Jock' to come to his office with me and he grilled him about exactly what tools he had had stolen. I just listened. 'Jock' wasn't as clever as he thought he was and Ian Lamont tied him up in knots as he constantly made contradictory claims. Lamont decided not to pay out either 'Jock' or Colin. Colin was rightly furious and so was I. I had 'Jock' in my office and lambasted him for ruining Colin's chance of getting his rightful compensation. Yet, he still insisted that he had had his tools stolen. Sometimes, working-class people can be their own worst enemies!

Don't get me wrong; I would have no qualms about falsely claiming something from employers if I could get away with it, because they are exploiting workers anyway, but I would never do so if it jeopardised a fellow worker getting the compensation that they rightly deserved. I continued to try to get Colin compensation, but his site agent, Graham, said that it had been taken out of his hands by Mr Lamont. Incidentally, Graham also showed his awareness of labour history when he described the incident as 'the builders' shilling (Colin Shilling), just like the dockers' tanner', but that was no consolation.

Another issue that I was constantly having to deal with was on Fridays when some workers would come back from the pub late after lunch, often having had too much to drink. Whilst I didn't condone it, I could understand that after working hard on a cold building site all morning, it was very appealing to stay in a nice warm pub for a bit longer. In the interests of safety though, I agreed with the company that they should not be allowed to go back out on site as they may put their fellow workers in danger. My response was that they should be put on one of the luxury coaches to sleep it off or, if they came with someone else who was sober, be sent home for the weekend and have the matter dealt with on the following Monday.

This view was shared by John Sheehan, the construction manager and Bill Kelly, the industrial relations officer; trying to discipline a drunk building worker never seemed like a good idea. Bill Longhurst, one of the site agents I mentioned earlier, was having none of it, though. He insisted that workers under his charge should be disciplined there and then, with the inevitable consequences; he was attacked, held up against the wall and punched by one drunk worker. Privately, both John Sheehan and Bill Kelly told me that they thought that the stupid idiot deserved it. Though I would never condone violence, I couldn't help but think the same.

As convenor of shop stewards negotiating for collective agreements with management wasn't the most difficult part of the job. Keeping all the workforce on our side was often trickier, especially when some of them had views that I found odious. There was a scaffolder foreman who supported all what the works committee were doing. He had been a trade union member for many years and had worked on the construction of several other power stations. So, I thought he was a good bloke. However, in a casual conversation with him one day, he suggested that 'you've got to give your missus a slap now and again just to keep her in order.' At first, I thought it was a sick joke, but when he insisted that he was deadly serious, I was horrified. I told him in no uncertain terms that I found his views on women totally obnoxious. Thankfully, and despite the stereotype of building workers to the contrary, such extreme macho, misogynistic attitudes were extremely rare both on the Littlebrook site and on building sites I worked on in general.

Also, one of the carpenters, Tommy, was a member of the National Front. I have to say that he wasn't very popular with the other carpenters because of this. However, when he had a personal issue that he needed help with from me, I did so as professionally as I could. I couldn't do otherwise. When he left my office, I had Jessie, the yard foreman who was a black guy from Grenada, come to see me to ask me why I was helping 'that racist bastard'. Now, I got on alright with Jessie. We'd often have long conversations about his homeland and he would bring me a bottle of rum back when he visited his folks in the Caribbean. I had to explain to him that showing no favouritism might just make Tommy see that we are all workers who should support one another. He wasn't convinced though.

Jessie was one of about a dozen black workers from the Caribbean who had worked for the company in South London for a while and were bussed to the site each day. There was probably a minority that engaged in covert racism towards them, but it was never in my presence and most other workers hated even minor demonstrations of racism because it undermined our collective spirit. Nevertheless, as a consequence of coming together on a bus and having known each other from previous sites, coupled with the general culture of racism that existed in society at the time, they tended not to fraternise with others on the site, preferring, for example, to socialise and sit together at lunch breaks. I always tried to involve them as much as possible in decision making, although their reluctance to mix with others on the site was understandable.

One exception was a gregarious carpenter and really good trade unionist known only as 'Mac'. On one occasion, Ian Lamont was standing watching Mac making up shutters in the yard. Mac stopped what he was doing and said in his strongest Caribbean accent 'Who you is man?' Lamont replied 'I am Mr Lamont, project manager.' Mac replied in his best received English accent 'Nice to meet you. I am Mr McCarthy, carpenter.' Everyone fell about laughing and loved Mac for his quirky sense of humour. Mac was one of many great characters on the site; characters such as 'Eric the s**t' (so-called because every time something went wrong, he would say 'Oh, I'm going for a s**t!'), 'the honey monster' and the aforementioned 'tatty head'. Dealing with all these different characters was sometimes a challenge, but was also a great experience.

Another carpenter was the son of the aforementioned site agent, Bill Longhurst. Some of the workers complained that he shouldn't be allowed to come into mass meetings because they couldn't express what they felt with him there, knowing that he'd only go and tell his dad. I said to them that I thought that was unfortunate if he did, but that as a worker and trade union member on site, he had every right to be there and that with so many workers on site, there was always going to be at least one person anyway who would feel the overwhelming need to go to management after meetings and blab to them about everything that had been discussed and who had said what.

I also told them that because of this I didn't tell them everything in mass meetings that the works committee were planning to do. Some workers, understandably, were unhappy with this, saying that keeping things from them was undemocratic. Terry, the steel fixer foreman who I shared a lift to work with, was particularly aggrieved about this and we had a long conversation in the car on the way home one night about this. My view generally was that I was only their representative and that I should share as much as I possibly could with them and that, though I might recommend courses of action, they were the ones that should decide what to do on the basis of knowing the full facts. However, this had to sometimes be balanced by the need to ensure that the management didn't get wind of what we were preparing to do. It was often a difficult balancing act to achieve and though it was sometimes necessary to keep things to myself, I didn't like doing it.

Chapter 6

What about 'Elf and Safety'?

I n the latter stages of my time on Littlebrook, health and safety became a more prominent issue. Before the Health and Safety at Work Act (1974) and its subsequent regulations, an average of 350 building workers lost their lives on sites every year and tens of thousands suffered life-changing injuries. Because of the legislation, and the activities of trade union activists in the guise of union-appointed safety reps., the death toll fell by the new century to about 50 a year; still 50 too many of course, but a vast improvement. Back in the 1970s, many people don't realise that the construction of a power station would, on average, claim seven lives and seriously injure many more. Yet today 'too much elf and safety!' is a fashionable media discourse that is often heard from the uninformed and right-wing politicians alike. Nigel Farage and many Tory politicians now claim that there is far too much 'red tape' and that many laws and regulations, and they usually include 'health and safety' laws in that, should be scrapped because they are 'crippling business'.

Well, these right-wingers need to be constantly reminded of the consequences for ordinary working people of proposals to cut health and safety legislation. One incident on the Littlebrook 'D' Power Station site in January, 1978 before the Safety Reps and Safety Committees Regulations (1977) came into force on 1st October 1978 should be enough to serve as a lesson on what 'cutting red tape' would mean in practice. A construction company by the name of *Edmund Nuttall Ltd* was contracted to dig the tunnel under the Thames to bring in water to run the turbines for the power station. Men worked underground and had to take a lift hoist down 200 feet to work on digging the tunnel.

Because the Safety Reps and Safety Committees regulations hadn't been enacted by then, shop stewards generally acted on behalf of workers in matters of health and safety. The shop steward for *Nuttall* reported several times to the company's management that he thought that the hoist was not being maintained properly and that it was dangerous. Instead of congratulating him on his diligence, the company threatened him with the sack if he kept complaining and holding up production.

On 9th January, 1978, nine workers got into the lift to go to start their shift. It should have been ten, but one worker had forgotten something and went back to get it, saying that he would get the next lift going down. The lift descended 50 feet before the cable snapped. As the lift sped up the safety brake should have come on, but it was fouled by lumps of hardened concrete. The lift plummeted 150 feet to the bottom, killing four workers and causing life-changing injuries to the other five.

As news spread around the site, every shop steward and every convenor steward from every other contractor, including myself, called their workers off the site so that the rescue squad could get on with their work unhindered. The rescue squad was made up of specialist workers from all the major contractors on site. I convened a meeting of the *Gleeson* works committee to discuss what to do. We decided to hold a mass meeting and recommend that everyone go home for the day, which was carried overwhelmingly. Before leaving with everyone else, I went to see Danny O'Connor, the convenor steward of *Laing's* and convenor of the Liaison Committee. He had called a meeting of his shop stewards committee and they had decided to do the same as us. We later learned that this was the same action that was taken by the workers with every other contractor on site.

Before leaving the site myself and while still in Danny O'Connor's office we heard that a news team, fronted by Trevor McDonald, had arrived on site. Although they were getting in the way of rescue vehicles arriving and leaving, there was no need for what happened next; one of *Laing's* shop stewards made a racist remark about Trevor McDonald. He was quite rightly verbally attacked and condemned by everyone present. I heard later that he had his shop steward's credentials withdrawn. Anyway, the news of the accident was the main story on *News at Ten* that evening.

When we returned to work the following day, we held a mass meeting in the canteen and decided to strike for the whole day on each of the days that the four funerals were held as a mark of respect for the workers who were killed as well as a protest against the health and safety record of construction companies. The Liaison Committee met and decided to start a collection from workers across all the contractors on site and also from other sites in Britain and across the world. It was decided unanimously at a mass meeting at *Gleeson's* for each worker to donate £10 per week for four weeks to support the widows of the four deceased workers and the five seriously injured ones.

To *Gleeson's* credit, they agreed with a proposal from me to deduct the £10 each week from every worker's wage packet under the guise of something else so they wouldn't pay tax on it as long as each worker signed an agreement for the company to do so; which everyone did. Money also came in from as far afield as Japan and a total of £56,000 was eventually raised and put into an account for the recipients to draw on.

The *Health and Safety Executive* subsequently charged *Nuttall* with six breaches of Health and Safety Regulations. When the case finally came to court, *Nuttall* were found guilty of five of those six **criminal** charges, but fined just £5000 on a contract where they were making millions. Nobody was sent to prison for what was effectively corporate murder. Compare that to the long prison sentences that the Shrewsbury pickets got on charges of affray that were trumped up anyway. No wonder that Marxists claim that the criminal justice system simply delivers a bourgeois version of 'justice'. The worst thing was that this wasn't the first time for *Nuttall*. They had already been involved in a similar incident a couple of years earlier on a site in Liverpool.

Anyway, from then on, the focus of struggles was very much on health and safety on site for the shop stewards and convenor stewards of all the contractors. In April 1978 fellow CPGB member, Bob Smith, got a start on the site as a labourer and he was a great ally in the fight over pay, conditions and particularly over health and safety issues with *Gleeson's*. Bob, having been forced to work on the lump most of his working life in appalling and dangerous conditions, was relatively unknown as a site activist and I guess that's why he managed to get a start, because it was clear that *Gleeson's* were refusing jobs to well-known trade union activists.

I know of at least two well-known activists who applied for jobs with *Gleeson's* and were turned down. One was the carpenter Fred West from Southend-on-Sea who was a CPGB member and who had been a very successful convenor steward at the Beckton sewerage works site. The other one was the bricklayer, Brian Higgins. When the blacklist held by the *Consulting Association* was finally uncovered in 2009, Brian's file was the biggest of all, running to 49 pages. I knew that they were both blacklisted because their names came up in casual conversation with management and the company admitted that they had both applied for jobs on the site. Yet, when I once mentioned the blacklist, I was met with howls of laughter and derision from management and told that we, trade union activists, were all paranoid. Bear this in mind for the revelation that comes later in this book.

As far as Bob Smith was concerned, when he started on the site, he came to see me and said that he could see that we had a well-organised works committee, didn't intend to try to muscle in and would give us any support that we needed. I said that it would be great if he could try to get sales of the *Morning Star* off the ground in the canteen at lunchtimes. He was very happy to perform this role and I supported him in that. Despite having a very pronounced stammer, Bob also frequently spoke very eloquently in mass meetings in support of recommendations that the works committee made. When his stammer got the better of him, he would sing his contribution which he could deliver without a hint of a stammer!

Back to the issue of health and safety. The Safety Reps and Safety Committees Regulations (1977) came into force on 1st October 1978 which, among other things, gave trade unions the right to appoint safety reps who would have certain rights and responsibilities in law. In other places of work trade unions appointed safety reps who were not shop stewards or union reps, but we felt that if the shop stewards on the works committee were also safety reps, they would be better protected from victimisation. The union issued four of us with credentials as safety reps. The legislation also enabled any safety rep to have paid time off to attend safety reps training either with their own trade union or with the TUC. All of us applied for, were accepted and attended TUC training courses one day a week for ten weeks. My course was at Barking College. The other reps went to courses near to their own homes.

As a consequence of our training we, as a works committee, agreed that as convenor, I would write a comprehensive proposal for a health and safety agreement to be put to management. In doing so I followed the regulations, codes of practice and guidance notes contained in the legislation, citing them as I went along and adapting them to suit our particular circumstances. Of course, the guidance notes are just that and don't have the same legal standing as the regulations or codes of practice. So, when we presented our proposals to management, they congratulated us, me in particular, on our well-written proposals (patronising bastards!) before rejecting them. What followed was lengthy negotiations over a number of weeks, with management trying to water down our proposals as much as they could; but this time we had the law on our side and they were forced to accept much more than they would have liked.

For the first time, we had provisions for regular inspections of the workplace. Each of us was responsible for different areas of the site that we would inspect fortnightly along with the appropriate site agents. Unlike most other workplaces, it is important to carry out inspections very frequently on building sites because they change so rapidly. We were all issued with carbonised reporting forms by our unions, with copies of what we observed going to the site agents for action. In addition, we had carbonised report forms to report one-off issues that both the relevant safety rep and relevant site agent would be required to sign.

At a mass meeting we encouraged all our members to not only report any health and safety issues verbally to their foremen or site agents, but also to report them to us, so that we could complete forms, get site agents to sign them and give them carbonised copies. Frank, the bricklayer shop steward, was particularly diligent in doing this for every issue, however small, that he came across or was reported to him. This infuriated some of the site agents because they resented the safety reps having the upper hand and because they knew that these forms would be used against them in proceedings if they didn't act swiftly on anything that was reported to them and an accident or illness occurred as a consequence.

After some lengthy negotiations with management, it was agreed to set up a safety committee comprising of four from the management side and the four trade union appointed safety reps. The four from the management side were Brian, the Deputy Project Manager, Bill Kelly, the industrial relations officer, the site agent Bill Longhurst, who I mentioned a number of times earlier, and the Site Safety Officer, Frank. Frank was the perfect example of the so-called 'Peter principle'. Before the Health and Safety at Work Act (1974) many large construction companies would appoint a member of management as the company or site safety officer because they had reached their level of incompetence. It was often regarded as a 'doddle of a job' with little responsibility.

Indeed, Frank was both incompetent and lazy. For example, when it came to monitoring exposure to fumes and vapours in certain areas of the site, it became clear that he didn't know how to do it. The safety reps had to show him how to do it because we had been trained how to do it on our TUC courses and he'd had no training in it whatsoever. Instead of being out on site most of the time, as he should have been, he spent most of his time in his nice warm office. On one occasion, the other Frank, the bricklayer shop steward and safety rep, walked into his office and found him asleep at his desk! Even the construction manager, John Sheehan, told me privately that he thought he was useless, but he wasn't his line manager and so couldn't do anything about it.

Anyway, it was agreed that responsibilities on the safety committee should be shared equally between management and safety reps. It was agreed that Brian, the Deputy Project Manager, would chair the safety committee and I would be the secretary. We felt that it was important that I took the role of secretary rather than the role of chair because I would get to write the minutes of the meetings and thus be able to ensure that what was recorded and how it was recorded would reflect our interests in pinning the company down to taking health and safety issues more seriously and as a permanent record of what had been agreed that the management had to do.

However, the biggest problem that we had with health and safety issues wasn't with *Gleeson's* but with the lack of coordination between contractors; mostly due to the incompetence of the client, the CEGB. In the main building in particular, the *Gleeson* workforce, led by Mick, the carpenter shop steward, walked off the site and sat in the canteen on a number of occasions because of material such as nuts and bolts, welding rods and showers of sparks dropping on their heads from above from other contractors. This was despite assurances given by the CEGB on several occasions that they had coordinated activities so that this couldn't happen.

Eventually, the workforce sat in the canteen and refused to go into the main building until something more permanent had been sorted out. The works committee met with Ian Lamont and other senior managers and thrashed out a deal for a volunteer task force of all trades to work an evening shift from 4.00pm until midnight when no other contractors would be there. The deal that was thrashed out was that those who volunteered would get 40p an hour extra on the basic rate for working unsocial hours and could volunteer for redundancy under a generous redundancy scheme that we had negotiated once the main building was completed, if they wanted to.

Furthermore, as there would be no senior managers working on the evening shift, only foremen, they would be set an amount of work to get done each evening that would ensure that the bonus that everyone on site got would not be affected. This worked fine, but what the task force started to do was to rush around getting all their set work done within two or three hours and then go off to the pub for the rest of the evening. They would take it in turns for one worker to stay on site in case there was an emergency and he had to call them back and also to clock them all off at midnight.

However, one evening, the aforementioned site agent, Bill Longhurst, decided to visit the site to see how work was progressing and was furious that, all bar one worker, they were down the pub. The following day I was called into the office to face Bill Longhurst, along with Bill Kelly, the industrial relations officer, to explain why they shouldn't all be given written warnings. My argument was that they'd been set a certain amount of work to get done and they'd done it. What was the problem? But, of course, that's not how capitalism works, is it. Nobody who supports the present way of organising society suggests that if an employer makes the profit that they had expected but then could make more by exploiting workers further, that they should be penalised for doing so! Anyway, they couldn't sack all of them, so it was left at 'tell them not to do it again!'

Meanwhile, the uncoordinated chaos continued on the site and the safety reps with other contractors were becoming increasingly angry and frustrated at the CEGB's lack of action. The Liaison Committee demanded that the CEGB set up a safety committee of safety reps and managers from all the contractors on site. Initially, the CEGB refused to do so. So, industrial action was directed by the workforces of several contractors at them. For example, the workforce of the steel erecting company, *Cleveland Bridge and*

Engineering Company, the most militant workforce on site, occupied the CEGB offices and even welded doors shut in the offices to stop managers from going into their offices.

Eventually, the CEGB relented and set up a coordinating safety committee of safety reps and managers from each of the main contractors on site. I attended meetings on behalf of the workforce of *Gleeson's* along with the deputy project manager, Brian. Both industrial relations and safety did improve on site after that. Probably as an act of self-congratulation, the CEGB commissioned a group of social scientists from the *Tavistock Institute of Human Relations* to examine the industrial relations record of the site. The social scientists had meetings with and interviewed CEGB managers, managers of all the main contractors, the Liaison Committee, all convenor stewards and six workers from each of the main contractors, chosen randomly.

Months later when we were given to understand that the final report had been written, the Liaison Committee requested a copy from the CEGB. The CEGB declined our request and said that they had decided not to publish it. Requests for copies from the *Tavistock Institute of Human Relations* were similarly declined with the reason given that they couldn't do so without permission from the CEGB. Many years later when I became a practising sociologist, I did a bit of digging and discovered that the CEGB had decided not to release the report because it was highly critical of CEGB managers and the respective managements of all the main contractors. They had reserved their praise for workers, their convenor stewards, their shop stewards and the Liaison Committee for doing everything in their power to improve industrial relations on site. No wonder the CEGB had decided not to publish it!

Despite these improvements, there were still problems with health and safety issues that we had to deal with on *Gleeson's*. For example, on one occasion, I had two of my carpenters come to my office to see me. They said that they had been asked to start cutting and fixing *Asbestolux* fire protection cladding. Now, at that time the asbestos industry was claiming that it was only blue asbestos that was dangerous and that *Asbestolux* sheeting made from white asbestos was safe. We weren't convinced. We immediately taped off the area and we all agreed to refuse to use it. *Gleeson* management, obviously concerned about any implications that might flow from insisting that we use it, requested that the company that had supplied it, remove it from site.

A couple of weeks later, the *Gleeson* management brought me a sample of a new product called *Supalux* that they claimed was safe to use. It looked similar to *Asbestolux* but had a slightly different finish. I said that I would get it tested. As a result of my TUC health and safety training, I had the contact details of a scientific laboratory in Sheffield that offered free services to trade unions. I sent the sample off to them and waited for the results. A week later I got their full report in the post that said that it was cement-based, not asbestos-based and was therefore no more hazardous than any other cement-based product that was used on building sites. I told the carpenters and they agreed with me that we could use it. I informed management.

A few days later a pallet load of sheets arrived. I inspected them and told the carpenters that they were *Supalux* and therefore okay to use. They set to work. About an hour later, the two carpenters came to see me and asked me to come and have a look at what they'd discovered. I went out on site and when I looked, I confirmed what they had suspected; the top six sheets on the pallet were indeed *Supalux*, but the rest of the pallet was *Asbestolux* sheets. We were furious that the supplier of this sheeting had tried to dupe us in that way. We immediately taped off the area and informed management. To be fair, *Gleeson's* management were equally furious, insisted that the supplier come and remove the pallet, cancelled their contract and got a new contractor to supply them. There was no trouble after that, but it just goes to show how workers have to be vigilant because in a capitalist society profit is invariably put before workers' health and safety.

The callousness of work in a capitalist society was demonstrated by another incident that happened. An older carpenters' labourer died from a heart attack on his way back from lunch one day. Although he was well-liked, he was a bit of a loner who had no close friends and no family, save for a son who lived in Leeds. His son came down to organise the funeral. It was decided that Mick, the carpenters' safety rep and myself would go to the funeral to represent his fellow workers and that the site agent, Bill Longhurst, and the safety officer, Frank, would go to represent management. On the day Mick and I brought our shirts, suits and ties to get changed into on site and we all went in Bill Longhurst's car to South London where the funeral was taking place. Apart from the deceased's son and his wife, we were the only four other people there. It was so sad.

After the funeral, the son invited us to come over to the pub across the road where he had laid on a few sandwiches for the wake. I could have gladly strangled Bill Longhurst when he declined the invitation, saying that he had to get me and Mick back to the site to get us back to work. The poor guy and his wife were left to mourn the loss of his father on their own. All the way back to the site I was cursing Bill Longhurst for his callousness, but also cursing myself for not sticking out and saying that if he wasn't staying for the wake then I would, that I would find my own way back afterwards and the company could stop my wages if they wanted. I think Mick felt the same.

Anyway, apart from incidents like that, everything was running much more smoothly up until Christmas 1978. However, the contract had passed its peak and after the Christmas break the company followed the letter of the law in informing us and negotiating with us about redundancies. By this time there were about 400 *Gleeson* workers on site. There would be no mass redundancies as there was still plenty of work to do, but each week I would be called into the office to be confronted with a list of the forthcoming redundancies in each trade. As I said earlier, we had negotiated a fairly generous redundancy package. We had also negotiated a last in-first out policy with regard to each trade after voluntary redundancies had been exhausted.

Nevertheless, we would always argue against the scale of the redundancies, even though this was on the basis of ignorance about staffing requirements; but we felt that it was important to register our extreme disapproval of the way that workers are simply discarded at the behest of employers in a capitalist society. The site agent, Bill Longhurst, unsurprisingly didn't see it like that. Every Friday when a new batch of redundancies were due to take place, those losing their jobs would go to the pub at lunchtime and come back rather worse for wear and not work in the afternoon.

Bill Longhurst was always furious about this and had me and other shop stewards in the industrial relations officer's office to tell us that this was not acceptable. He said: 'When I was on the tools, we got just half an hour to sharpen our tools before finishing time when we were laid off!' Frank, the bricklayer steward, in his usual sharp-witted way, replied 'Yes, but there's been two world wars since then Bill.' Longhurst was unperturbed and continued with 'where's their loyalty to the company', seemingly oblivious to the fact that the company had shown no loyalty to the workers that they had just sacked. I pointed out that if the company had shown any loyalty at all to the workers that had made huge profits for *Gleeson's*, they would have offered them transfers to other *Gleeson* sites. This was like water off a duck's back, but at least Bill Kelly, the industrial relations officer, could see the irony. Nothing ever came of this because how could Longhurst discipline someone who was leaving the employ of *Gleeson's* that day anyway?

One Friday in January 1979, I was called to Bill Kelly's office. I entered without knocking. On his desk was a copy of the *Morning Star* open on the letters page where I spotted a letter from Bob Smith, the labourer and CPGB member who had started on site in April 1978 and who had been a loyal supporter of the works committee and all that we were trying to do. Kelly quickly slammed the paper shut. He then proceeded to give me a list of 10 labourers who were due to be made redundant in the next tranche of redundancies. They were in order of last in-first out and last one on the list was Bob Smith. I could see what was happening and I argued strongly that at that time there was no need for as many as ten to go, but he was adamant. Bob had clearly been targeted and, indeed, there were no more redundancies of labourers for a couple of months after that.

Other than that, the redundancies were a very slow trickle that went on for months. One day in the summer of 1979, Ian Lamont asked to see me and the rest of the works committee in his office. He put it to us that he wanted to agree a fixed hourly bonus in order to avoid the weekly round of negotiations. There were conditions, though. Firstly, he asked that our three shop stewards who regularly negotiated with the bonus clerk and the site agents continued to collect detailed information about delays to our work through no fault of our own so that he could claim for the delays from the CEGB. We had no problem with our shop stewards giving information on delays to work in progress to management if it benefitted the workers we represented on site; after all, our primary purpose as shop stewards was to get the best wages and conditions that we could for our members.

The second condition was that, being as we now had agreements on all the major issues including the bonus scheme, health and safety and a redundancy package, that I should go back on the tools. Although I could no longer justify being a full-time convenor and, indeed, felt guilty at times that I wasn't having to work as hard as the members I represented on site, I was concerned that if issues arose that I needed time off from work for that there would be no barriers put in my way. I was given assurances in this regard and assurances that all site agents and foremen would be instructed accordingly.

However, all this depended on what was being offered as a fixed bonus rate. As the job was past its peak, it was getting more and more difficult to keep the bonus above £2.30 an hour. After lengthy negotiations, we settled on £2.10 an hour which we thought as a works committee was worth recommending to the workforce because, unlike what we had been earning, which was falling anyway, it was guaranteed. We put this to a mass meeting in the canteen and it was accepted overwhelmingly. Indeed, many workers congratulated us, both during and after the meeting, and thanked us for how well we'd done.

So, back to work on the tools I went. By this time there was very little shuttering work left to do and most of the work I had to do was second fixing; something that I was most comfortable with as I had done so much of it before. Most of the work was hanging big one-hour fire-check doors. Those of us that were doing this work worked independently of each other in separate rooms. It was precision work as the doors had fire-expansion strips all round that would completely seal rooms if a fire started. It was the kind of work that I was good at, having worked in high-class joinery workshops.

After a few days a couple of the carpenters came to see me and said that the other carpenters were all concerned that I was doing a bit too much and asked me to slow down as it was making it look bad for the rest of them. I said that after three years off the tools squeezing everything that I could out of the company for everybody's sake that I had to be careful because I was probably being monitored very closely and the company were looking for any excuse to discipline me. They said: 'Look Jack, you shouldn't worry about that. We've got your back and we're speaking on behalf of all the carpenters. If they try it on with you again, we've already all agreed that we'll all just walk off the site again.' I thanked them for their continued support and said that I would slow down a bit. It was really good to be back with the lads on site and experience that sense of everyday solidarity.

That wasn't the end of industrial action though. During that summer there was a big push on to improve wages and conditions nationally. During the middle years of the 1970s the

UK inflation rate had soared, reaching 24% in 1975. It was still 16% in 1977 and the basic rate of pay hadn't kept up. Negotiations with the employers nationally had been going nowhere and an appeal went out from UCATT for members to put pressure on the employers to make a more realistic offer. As the day of final negotiations in London approached, we held a mass meeting, decided to strike for the day and as many of us as possible to go to central London to lobby the talks.

On the day, I couldn't believe how well-supported our action was. There were still about 250 *Gleeson* workers left on the site and 100-150 of them went to central London and lobbied the talks, congregating in the road outside chanting and singing for the whole afternoon. I did become a little bit worried though when a few of them, fuelled by too much alcohol, broke into the building and occupied some of the upper floors, hanging out of the windows and whipping up the crowd. There were many others there, including Danny O'Connor from *Laing's* on our site and from other sites as well, but I'm pretty sure that our demonstration must have had some effect, with the employers fearing a repeat of 1972 because, although the claim for a reduced working week wasn't achieved, a more than 17% increase in basic pay was.

In late summer of 1979 we decided as a works committee that before workers had left in great number, we would hold a social; an early 'topping out' party if you like. We managed to hire the social club of the existing Littlebrook Power Station for a Saturday night and invited all present and past *Gleeson* workers on the site to bring their wives and partners for a social gathering. We also invited the full-time organisers from the TGWU and UCATT, including the Regional Secretary, Len Eaton, from the latter. We booked a disco and ordered 200 portions of chicken and chips from *Kentucky Fried Chicken* to be delivered to the venue on the night. Vegetarianism was rare in those days and veganism was virtually unknown, so that was no problem. It was a great evening and everyone said how much they enjoyed it.

Chapter 7

Moving on to pastures new.

Back on site the trickle of redundancies continued for the rest of 1979. By Christmas there was still about 200 of us left. So, into 1980 many of the lads were keeping half an eye out for other jobs, but as I was well-down the list of carpenters to go, I wasn't that concerned to look for other work for a while. Then, one evening in March I got a phone call from the London Regional Secretary of UCATT, Len Eaton, telling me that *Bovis Construction Ltd* were starting work on a new development at Piccadilly Circus that was spread right up to Wardour Street between Shaftsbury Avenue and Coventry Street, principally taking in the original *Lyons Corner House* and the *Golden Nugget* casino. It was to be a major development of shops, arcades, futuristic elevators, the *Pepsi Max Drop*, theatres, cinemas and *Sega World*, collectively to be known as the *Trocadero*.

He said that the site would need organising and he thought that I'd be the best person for the job. He asked me if I would apply for a job as a carpenter there. I was a bit sceptical at first because Len was a right-winger and I had proven to be quite militant. Nevertheless, I think he realised that, although we differed in our views and our approaches, I was never a 'hothead'. I decided to trust him when he said that he had confidence in me being the best person for the job. He gave me the contact details of the site agent, Geoff, and I arranged to go for an interview with him. I took the day off work, went for the interview and was offered the job. It was National Working Rule Agreement wages and conditions, everyone on site was properly employed and there was a collective bonus scheme for each trade. I agreed to start a week later as I had to give a week's notice at Littlebrook in order to qualify for the voluntary redundancy package.

When I went back into work the following day, I went straight to the industrial relations officer's office and volunteered for redundancy, which was gratefully accepted. For fear that it might jeopardise my start with *Bovis*, I told neither him nor anyone else on site where I was going. I went back out on site to get on with my work. Within a couple of hours, I was told that Ian Lamont, the director and project manager, wanted to see me in his office. I went alone because I couldn't see the point in me taking another shop steward with me anymore.

As I entered his office, he said to me: 'So, you're going to work for *Bovis* then, are you?' I didn't ask him how he knew because it was obvious that *Bovis* had contacted him for a reference. We were on our own, so I said: 'You bastard, you wouldn't put in a bad word for me, would you?' With a grin on his face, he replied: 'No, I'm delighted that you're going to work for one of my rivals. I'll be glad to see the back of you.'
Nevertheless, one evening during my one week's notice, I got a phone call at home from Peter Hutchinson, the director of *Bovis* with responsibility for industrial relations. He told me that they had checked up on me and had had second thoughts about offering me a job. When I asked him why, he simply said that they didn't think I was suitable. I asked him what wasn't suitable about me and what was I supposed to do now, as I had already handed in my notice and this represented a breach of trust. He said 'sorry' and hung up. I immediately rang the London Regional Secretary of UCATT, Len Eaton, and told him. He said: 'Leave it with me.'

About an hour later, Peter Hutchinson rang me again and said: 'We've had a change of heart and you can start on the site next Monday.' I immediately rang Len Eaton and asked him what he had said to Hutchinson. He told me that he said to Hutchinson that if I wasn't allowed to start on the job on Monday morning, *Bovis* would see a picket surrounding their site of workers from every major site in London. Whether or not he did say this or actually said and agreed something else is a moot point. You see, I still couldn't fully trust him.

Back at the Littlebrook site, I called a meeting of the carpenters, told them I was leaving and asked for nominations to replace me as shop steward for the carpenters. Colin was proposed, seconded and voted in. I was quite pleased that my role as shop steward for the carpenters was being left in such capable hands. Colin was a good trade unionist who had supported the works committee throughout his time on the site. We then held a meeting of all the shop stewards to inform them and to elect a new convenor steward. The meeting decided that Colin would make a good convenor steward because he was militant, but was a sensible choice, unlike one or two of the others who were rather more hot-headed.

We then held a mass meeting where I thanked everyone for their support over the years and assured them that the trade union organisation on site was being left in safe hands. Management was informed and we applied for credentials for Colin from the UCATT office. I then spent a day showing Colin the ropes and going through all the documents and agreements that we had with management. Seeing the details of all the agreements we had made over the previous four years, Colin said that he was amazed at how well we'd done. He vowed to do everything in his power to defend and, where possible advance, all that we had achieved together.

I took all my tools home on the Thursday night because I knew that I would be spending Friday morning tying up loose ends, for example with the Liaison Committee. I went to work in someone else's car. As everyone who left did on their last day, I went to the pub at lunchtime. The pub was packed with *Gleeson* workers who seemingly all wanted to buy me a drink. As pints, whiskeys and rums piled up on the table in front of me, that was the last I remember until the following day when I woke up fully clothed on my own bed at home at about lunchtime with a massive hangover!

Apparently, in the early evening of that Friday Sue had noticed a car keep going up and down our turning in Aveley. The turning was a dead end. Eventually the occupants of the car knocked at our door and when Sue opened it, there were two men who she'd never seen before holding me up blind drunk between them saying 'are you Mrs Fawbert?' They said that they knew that I lived in that road but weren't sure of the number and had been knocking on doors up and down the street until someone had told them where I lived.

They took me straight upstairs and left me on the bed. My son Paul was only five at the time and Sue said later that he was really worried and kept saying: 'Is Daddy alright?' Before leaving, one of the two men gave Sue a brown packet that had all my week's wages, my redundancy money and my week's pay in hand in it totalling £925; a massive sum in 1980. He told Sue that they'd taken it off me in case I lost it or had it stolen. To this day I still don't know who they were, but I am eternally grateful for their kindness in taking me home and their honesty.

On the following Monday morning I arrived bright and early on the *Bovis* site in Piccadilly carrying my tools. The hours were 8.00am until 4.30pm, but most workers were starting at 7.30am and finishing at 6.00pm; that is half an hour overtime in the mornings and one and a half hours overtime at the end of the day. This meant that I had to leave home at 6.00am to drive to Barking, park my car and get the overground train to Fenchurch Street station, walk from there to Tower Hill underground station to get the tube to Piccadilly Circus, changing at Charing Cross, and then walk to the site. It also meant that I didn't get home most nights until at least 7.30pm just as the kids were going to bed.

Most of the workers on site were also working Saturdays as overtime, making it 6 times 10 hour days; in other words, 60 hours a week. Sometimes, overtime was also offered for Sundays. I didn't have to do it, but being as the bonus was much lower than I had been used to at Littlebrook, initially I chose to. I had a young family and a mortgage to pay. After a short induction and introduction to site management, I walked out onto the floor of the old *Lyons Corner House* to be greeted with a cheer and someone shouting 'Hurrah, Jack Fawbert's here! We're in the money! We're in the money!'

It was a carpenter called Johnny who had worked on the Littlebrook site for *Gleeson* where he had been affectionately known as 'Johnny Rotten' or sometimes 'motormouth'. I went up to him and greeted him but told him to keep quiet and cool it; I still had my week's probation to serve. He apologised and agreed to say nothing to anyone else on site for a week or so. Later that morning I was approached by the convenor of shop stewards, a West Indian carpenter called Vic, who asked me if I was in the union. I had brought my union card with me and I got it out of my pocket and showed him. He seemed taken aback because most of the workers on the site, including himself, were on check-off (their union dues were collected by the employer) and I don't think he was sure what he was looking at.

Anyway, I got my head down and for the next couple of weeks and I said little. One day, the UCATT full-time official, Dominic Hehir, came on site. He approached me in the canteen at lunchtime, introduced himself and gave me a note from Alf Alden, the UCATT official that covered Littlebrook. He said that Alf had a case going to an industrial tribunal at ACAS the following week and wanted me to come along as a witness. I would get paid expenses and loss of earnings. I didn't know anything about the case and assumed that Alf would brief me before proceedings began, so I agreed to go. Knowing what Alf was like from my dealings with him on the Littlebrook site, I should have known better.

When I got to the tribunal hearing, I discovered that it was two carpenters from Littlebrook who were claiming unfair selection for redundancy on the basis that they were two of the best carpenters on site. They clearly had no case because, as I said earlier, we had an agreement for last in, first out. As we filed into the courtroom, I sat immediately behind the two carpenters and Alf. Just before proceedings were about to commence, Alf turned round to me and said: 'So, what do you want me to say?' I was gobsmacked! He had no idea what he was doing. He had clearly not read the redundancy agreement that we had on site and had clearly prepared nothing for the case. I just said: 'I don't know, why are you asking me?' and he fumbled his way through a half-cocked, off the hoof claim.

When I was called to give evidence, I resolved that I would just tell the truth. The two carpenters knew what the site agreement was and I wasn't going to perjure myself for an incompetent idiot like Alden. When asked, I confirmed that there was a site agreement for last in, first out in each trade and that, as far as I was aware, the two carpenters were the next two in line to go. The case was dismissed and Alf was lucky that the tribunal judge didn't make an order for *Gleeson* to recover costs for unreasonable conduct. Alf seemed oblivious to his own incompetence, simply saying to the two carpenters as we left: 'Oh well, we tried.' It was also clear that Alf had encouraged the two carpenters to make a claim.

Back at the *Bovis* site, Johnny and a few other carpenters who I knew from previous sites were pressing for Vic to call a meeting, because they wanted me to take over as their shop steward. I wasn't happy about this because I thought it would create ill-feeling between the carpenters and especially between Vic and myself. Vic wasn't a 'company man' as such, but he had only worked for *Bovis* for years and had been transferred from site to site as 'the convenor steward' as a 'safe pair of hands'; a practice that a number of companies in London followed to try to avoid 'trouble' on their sites. So, when a meeting of the carpenters was eventually called and someone suggested replacing Vic with me, I said that Vic was doing a good job and suggested that we approach the site agent, Geoff, to see if he would agree to there being a second carpenter shop steward as Vic would be busy with duties as the convenor steward. The meeting agreed, we approached Geoff, who agreed, and I became the carpenter shop steward.

At a subsequent works committee meeting Vic said that I seemed to know what I was doing much more than he did and suggested that I take over as the convenor steward. The meeting agreed, but I said that I would only do so if Vic remained as the carpenter shop steward because I valued his support. He agreed to do this. The full-time official, Dominic Hehir, was informed and he visited the site to see me. He knew that Len Eaton, the Regional Secretary, who of course was a right-winger, had engineered getting me on the site. As a CPGB member, Dominic was wary of me at first, until I assured him that my political affiliation and views were the same as his.

As far as site conditions were concerned, they were pretty good. Indeed, *Bovis* had a reputation as being one of the best amongst the large construction companies for providing good welfare facilities. There were decent toilets, changing rooms and a canteen serving hot food. The company even negotiated the price of food in the canteen with shop stewards and then invited private companies to bid for the work at those prices. Protective clothing, such as donkey jackets and safety equipment, such as helmets, were top notch and they even supplied tee shirts for workers to wear on site in the summer. Though not perfect, safety was a much higher priority than for some contractors that I had worked for previously.

The site agent, Geoff, was very accommodating with regard to employment practices and relations with the trade unions. Although there was far too much work subcontracted out for my liking, he did insist on workers of all subcontractors being properly employed on the cards and being members of the appropriate trade unions. He would inform me when new subcontractors came on site, so that I could check them out and make sure that they were all trade union members.

On one occasion, a new plastering subcontractor told me that none of his men were trade union members and that they didn't intend to join anyway. I told him they had to and he said that I couldn't make them. I told him that was true, but that the site agent could. He didn't believe me, so I told Geoff. He must have spoken to them because shortly afterwards, the boss of the subcontractor came to see me, took a large wad of notes out of his back pocket and said: 'How much do you want then?' I told him in no uncertain terms that it didn't work like that. He protested that other union officials had taken the money in the past. Whether this was true or not, I don't know, but I reported this to Geoff and, fair play to him, he told them to get off his site.

Like at *Gleeson's* the bonus scheme was the biggest bone of contention. For carpenters the bonus being paid out most weeks was about 80p an hour and it was similar for the other trades and the labourers. Most of the work was one-off bespoke work and so the bonus clerk, Bob, was left to estimate each job as it came along. It was pretty clear that, on the orders of his superiors, he was manipulating the figures to make sure that the bonus came out at roughly the same for each trade each week.

I decided that I would challenge his figures with regard to the carpenters' bonus. However, before I did, I saw that the TUC were offering a course on work study at West Ham College and I thought that it would be a good idea to go on this course first. I applied, was accepted and given time off by *Bovis* to attend. The tutor was a great bloke called Norman Newton who was an active trade unionist himself who loved helping other trade unionists. Norman was to become a significant figure in my career development.

Back at the site and armed with my new found knowledge, I approached Bob one week and asked him if I could check the bonus sheets for the carpenters. At first, he seemed affronted at what he thought was my audacity at questioning his competence and said 'why?' I simply replied 'because I have a right to.' I went through them with a fine toothcomb and found that some things that the carpenters had done were not recorded on the sheets and that some targets were grossly unfair. I challenged him about these 'errors' and thus started the weekly ritual of negotiating over his 'calculations'. Every week I'd be in his office arguing over the bonus for hours on end. One day he said to me 'will you ever be satisfied?' I replied: 'Not until we get £2.00 an hour bonus.' He said: 'Well, you'll never get that.' 'We'll see' I simply replied.

I know Bob was only an employee doing a job just like me, but he was the face of management that I had to grind down. On a couple of occasions his boss Brian came down to the site to try to, as he saw it, 'reason with me', but I wasn't relenting. Bob had given up smoking and had decided to just have a couple of cigars each day, but within a few months he was continually puffing away on a cigar. The bonus gradually rose until it got to about £2.00 an hour most weeks, but I had to keep challenging his figures every week to keep it at that level. There was one job, fixing joists, that became an ongoing battle because in some circumstances, it was easy and quick to do so, but in other circumstances it was much more difficult and took much longer.

I encouraged the shop stewards for the other trades and for the labourers to do what I had been doing and they did so with varying degrees of success. The most successful one was Viv, the labourers' shop steward, who I became particularly friendly with. We'd sometimes go for a pizza after work, visit the National Gallery and go to lectures at the Marx Memorial Library in the evening. All this pressure must have got to Bob because he said to me privately one week: 'If I make the carpenters' bonus come out to roughly £2.00 an hour every week, will you leave me alone?' I agreed to do as he asked.

Everything was fine after that for a few months and then the bonus started dropping by small amounts each week. When the bonus dipped to £1.80 one week, I went into Bob's office and said that I wanted to start checking the sheets again. He said 'I thought we had an agreement that you wouldn't?' I reminded him that that private arrangement was conditional. I'd kept my side of the bargain, but he hadn't kept his side of it by making the bonus come out to roughly £2.00 an hour each week. After that I continued to check the sheets and negotiate changes with him for the rest of my time on the site. Mick, who had been such an effective shop steward and bonus negotiator at Littlebrook, started on the site and he became a great confidante and supporter.

Whilst the bonus issue was important, there were other issues of a more general nature that loomed large. A Tory government under Margaret Thatcher's leadership committed to right-wing monetarist policies had been elected in 1979. By early 1981 unemployment had soared as a result. A march of some 500 people was planned to go from Liverpool to London to protest about this scourge. It was to be called 'The People's March for Jobs'. It was going to cost in the region of £70,000 to clothe and feed the marchers.

So, a nationwide appeal was made for funds and for people to sign the petition. I invited veteran construction union activist and Communist Party industrial organiser, Tom Durkin, to come to speak about the march in the canteen on the site. He was brilliant!

Though far from being a spring chicken, Tom jumped up on one of the tables in the canteen and gave a rousing speech that had the whole canteen cheering. Everyone signed the petition and several workers gave money for the event.

I also took up other issues with *Bovis* from time to time. In mid-1981, I had read in the trade press and in the *Morning Star* that the works committee on Camden Council Direct Labour department had negotiated an equal opportunities agreement with the council to give women and girls job opportunities on their construction sites. They had subsequently employed a number of girls and women as apprentices in painting and decorating, bricklaying, carpentry, plumbing etc.

I thought to myself that if they could do it in the public sector, why couldn't I try to get such an agreement with *Bovis* in the private sector? If I could, I would be the first to do so with a major construction contractor. It seems crazy now but at that time I'd never seen a female building worker on any site that I'd worked on, save for one or two site engineers. Yet, just a generation earlier during the second world war when most young men were away in the forces, women worked in the construction industry in large numbers. Indeed, by 1944, 25,000 women were doing so. Some sites even had a majority of workers who were female e.g. 65 per cent of the workforce that built the new Waterloo Bridge during the war were women. Thames riverboat pilots even used to call it 'the Ladies Bridge'.

Yet, most of this history was hidden for a long time after the war as a mass propaganda campaign by the government was launched to force women to return to their 'traditional' roles as homemakers and carers, so that jobs were available for men returning from the front. 'A woman's place is in the home' became the establishment mantra as records of women working during the war, particularly in the construction industry, were destroyed or covered up by referring to them in documents by euphemisms such as 'green workers'. By the 1970s most building workers had no idea that women had made such a vital contribution to the war effort. This hidden history was only revealed through the sterling work of several social historians, particularly Christine Wall (Clarke & Wall, 2015).

Using the Sex Discrimination legislation as a guide, I drew up a proposal to put to management. The director in charge of industrial relations, Peter Hutchinson, came down to the site and together with the other shop stewards, Geoff the site agent and other members of management, we thrashed out a deal that just required a few minor tweaks to what I'd proposed. In fact, the company were quite enthusiastic about reaching an agreement. They were certainly more progressive than many of the building contractors that I'd worked for previously. The main provision included strategies to encourage girls to apply for apprenticeships with the company.

The biggest problem I had was not with negotiating such a deal with management, but with selling it to workers in a mass meeting on site. At that time there was, and probably still is to some extent, a chauvinistic, macho culture amongst a significant minority of building workers; as I said earlier. The site was very close to the Soho area, (in)famous for its sex shops and strip clubs. One carpenter, Chris, for example, used to spend his lunch break at a 'peep show' in Soho looking through a hole at women undressing. It was his 'little treat' he used to say.

The area around Piccadilly and Soho where the site was situated also afforded some of them the opportunity to stereotypically stand on scaffolds wolf-whistling at young women as they passed; though it has to be said that the majority of workers thought that these Neanderthals were just 'dick-heads'. Some of them got their comeuppance once when they wolf-whistled what they thought was an attractive young woman. It turned out to be the famous drag artist Danny La Rue who embarrassed them with replies that they hadn't bargained for!

Anyway, at the meeting to discuss the equal opportunities agreement, some workers made the usual arguments that were around at the time that women were not strong enough to do many of the jobs that men did on sites. My response was to say that the maximum weight that workers were permitted to lift by law on sites was equivalent to the weight of a five-year-old child and were they seriously suggesting that no mother ever picks up their five-year-old child? To that, some workers retorted that that may be the case, but, as everyone knows, building workers do pick up much heavier weights than permitted by law. I replied: 'Yes, and no wonder so many building workers suffer from back problems!'

The other argument was that women wouldn't put up with the poor welfare, poor sanitary conditions and awful toilets that exist on most sites. My response was: 'If women wouldn't tolerate such conditions, why should you? If we had women on sites, the facilities just might improve then. Are you against that?' Anyway, thankfully, the overwhelming majority of workers voted to accept the agreement. Unfortunately, I never stayed long enough with *Bovis* to see any girls or women being taken on by the company.

The reason was that I was about to embark on a course of action that in the end would result in a rather dramatic career change. I applied for and was accepted on another TUC day release course at West Ham College with Norman Newton. I can't remember what the course was, but during the course Norman handed out leaflets advertising a one-year full-time course at the Enfield campus of Middlesex Polytechnic entitled the Certificate in Industrial Relations and Trade Union Studies (CIRTUS). The course was validated by the Council for National Academic Awards (CNAA), the national degree-awarding authority in the UK until its dissolution in 1993. He encouraged all the students to apply, but particularly targeted me and another student.

He said that we could apply to our respective local authorities for a grant similar to the grant that was given at the time for undergraduate study and that many local authorities, particularly Labour controlled ones, would give such a grant. Furthermore, he said that most of the students who succeeded on the course then went on to study at undergraduate level. At first I rejected the idea out of hand because I didn't consider myself to be academic and I couldn't see myself surviving on a grant, especially as I had a mortgage to pay and a wife and two children to support. I thought it wouldn't be fair on them.

However, I just happened to mention it to Sue and she said that she had been keen on moving up to Lakenheath in Suffolk where her sister and her husband had moved to and that it might be possible to do this if, after doing the CIRTUS course, we could relocate there and I could be accepted onto a degree course in Cambridge, Norwich or somewhere within daily travelling distance of Lakenheath. She reckoned that we could sell our home and get one much cheaper and better in Lakenheath and still have money in the bank to help see us through the three years at university.

I immediately became more enthusiastic about applying for the course as a precursor to studying at degree level, especially as the site agent at *Bovis* had told me that I would have difficulty getting a job on any other major site after this one. Whether he was trying to tip me off that I was on the blacklist or threatening me, I'm still not sure, but either way, I knew that my future would be uncertain if I decided to try to stay in the construction industry. I had this vague idea that after completing the CIRTUS course and a degree that I could try to get a graduate job doing something in the labour movement.

It was also the case that during student holidays I could either work as a carpenter or sign on for unemployment benefit, because I had previously worked, as well as getting rate rebates, free school meals for the children and so on. So, I applied for a place on the course. I, along with other applicants, was asked to come along for a full day of activities, introduction to the course and the campus, tests and individual interviews. The course leader was Alan Richardson, an active trade unionist himself who made all of the applicants feel welcome. I remember that one of the tests we were all asked to do was to write a short essay in a fixed amount of time on one from a number of questions related to industrial relations. It wasn't too 'heavy' as the idea was just to gauge the level of our literacy skills. I wrote my short essay on a question about the Safety Reps and Safety Committees Regulations.

Anyway, I was accepted onto the course. The next thing I needed to do was to apply to my local authority, Thurrock District Council, for a grant. I was really disappointed when I received a letter back from them refusing me a grant. I mentioned this to Larry Spector, a Labour Party member and fellow building worker who I talked about earlier. Larry said to leave it with him and he would speak with Tony Banks, Greater London Council Labour councillor who was later to become an MP, to see if there was anything he could do. Shortly after that, Tony Banks contacted me and advised me to move from the Aveley branch of UCATT to the Barking and Dagenham branch and to apply for a grant to Barking and Dagenham Council. He said that he would support my application if I did.

I duly did this and was indeed offered a grant by Barking and Dagenham Council. However, it wasn't a full grant, though. It was only £925 for the year, but what it meant was that my fees would also be paid by the council and I could apply for a number of other benefits. Also, Larry, who was a member of the Barking and Dagenham branch of UCATT, proposed to the branch that they also provide me with some financial support, arguing that as trade unionists we should support the education of our own. Whilst it was only a small grant, it all helped and I am very grateful to Larry to this day for all the help and assistance that he gave me. I am also very grateful to all of the members of the Barking and Dagenham branch of UCATT for voting unanimously to support Larry's proposal.

The only way I could repay the branch's generosity was that for the next year or so I contributed as much as I could in terms of attendance and contributions to debates in the branch. Dad was chair of the branch, having stepped down as secretary after 25 years of loyal service. So, there were now two CPGB members in the branch. One point to note about that time was that the *Daily Express* ran a front-page story criticising the 'communist-dominated branch' for passing a motion to go forward to the Labour Party conference calling for unilateral nuclear disarmament. The article questioned why communists should be allowed to determine Labour Party policy. What the article didn't mention was that the motion was proposed by Larry Spector, a Labour Party member, and seconded by another Labour Party member. Dad and I had nothing to do with framing the motion or proposing it, but why should the *Daily Express* let these details get in the way of a good 'reds under the bed' story?

Anyway, I waited until a week before the CIRTUS course started at Middlesex Polytechnic before handing in my notice to *Bovis*. I had been there just 18 months. I think Bob, the bonus clerk, was the most relieved person on the site! Everyone wished me well, but I think most of the management team were glad to see the back of me! With the help of Mick, who had done such a great job at Littlebrook, Vic took over 'policing' the bonus scheme and he also resumed his position as convenor steward. I would like to think that he was much wiser as a convenor steward than when he had held the position previously; not that I was, in today's parlance, a great influencer.

Chapter 8

From carpenter to student and back again!

It was September 1981 when I started the CIRTUS course at Middlesex Polytechnic. The course contained a number of different subjects (they didn't call them 'modules' in those days) including the core subjects of industrial relations, industrial sociology, labour history and labour law; all taught by different lecturers. Students could then choose options including economics, politics and philosophy. There was also an optional weekly class in English for those who felt that they needed some help with their literacy skills. I felt that I, in particular, needed these extra classes that were taught by a very sympathetic and enthusiastic lecturer called Jane and I attended each week.

Other lecturers on the course were an inspiration to me. Alan, the course leader, was an ex-manual worker who showed great empathy with students, particularly with the ex-manual workers on the course. John Crutchley, who taught industrial sociology, seemed to have a chaotic private life, and because he lived in Brighton, often sleeping in his office and looking like he had done so when he turned up for lectures. He had long, hippy-style hair and had a dishevelled appearance. He also sometimes brought his baby daughter into lectures in her pushchair and left her in the corner of the room while giving the most brilliant lectures off-the-cuff. When he didn't have his daughter with him, he would often adjourn seminars to the student bar where debates would go on for hours, especially after we'd all had a few pints!

Of the other lecturers, the one that was the greatest inspiration to me was a history teacher, Clive Fleay, from a local school who, one day a week came to the college to teach what was his passion; labour history, something that he never got the opportunity to do at school. Clive was only young, but he looked like the stereotypical secondary school history teacher with his pudding basin haircut, leather elbow patches on his jacket and corduroy trousers. However, appearances can be deceptive. Clive was so enthusiastic about his subject that his enthusiasm inevitably rubbed off on most of his students; me in particular. Labour history has been a passion of mine ever since.

Students on the course came from a very wide spectrum of the labour movement. There were train drivers, miners, secretarial workers, nurses and building workers like myself. There were also one or two graduates who were taking the course as a post-graduate qualification. The course was run like a traditional undergraduate course with lectures, seminars for which we had reading lists, and occasional one-to-one tutorials. Assessment was by essays for which we were given titles and reading lists. There was also a 5,000-word project that students could choose the subject of in consultation with their allocated supervisor. It had to be submitted at the end of the year.

I did my project on 'The Trade Union as Employer' looking at how trade unions treat their own employees in terms of salaries and conditions. I used mostly secondary sources, but I did go out to interview employees of a few trade unions. It wasn't very systematic and rigorous and I was rather anecdotal, mainly because I stupidly didn't make full use of my supervisor, Gerry, the economics lecturer, to discipline my study more. Nevertheless, I produced some useful results showing that some trade unions were much better employers than the ones that their officials had to deal with in the sectors that they covered. However, I was horrified to find that some major trade unions were terrible employers and treated their employees abysmally and, indeed, treated them far worse than what they would have expected from the public and private companies that their officials had to negotiate with in their work.

During the course, I managed to supplement our income with some private cash-in-hand jobs at weekends. One such private job was really unexpected. To my surprise, I got a call one weekend from Peter Hutchinson, the industrial relations director at *Bovis* who had initially tried to block me from getting started on the Piccadilly redevelopment, asking me if I could make two traditional sliding sash windows in non-standard sizes for him for an old cottage that he had bought. He knew that I was a good joiner and so he knew that he would get a good job.

As I was no longer working for *Bovis*, I agreed, but I told him that I wouldn't be doing him any favours and that I would charge him commercial rates. I also said that he would have to arrange to come and pick them up from my garage when I'd finished them. I made sure that I made a really good job of them because, as anyone who has read *The Ragged Trousered Philanthropists* will know, it is important to show employers that for skilled workers, good craftmanship counts for far more than making a profit. Also, my dad's old adage that active trade unionists should always try to be above reproach when it came to their professionalism, was uppermost in my mind.

Near the end of the CIRTUS course, we were given help by Jane in applying for places in Higher Education. At that time there were two systems; UCCA for applying for university places and PCAS for applying for degree courses at colleges and polytechnics. They have since been amalgamated to form UCAS. Anyway, as we were moving to Lakenheath in Suffolk, I wanted a course where I could travel daily. Higher Education provision was pretty sparse in East Anglia at the time, so on the UCCA application I just applied for Politics and Economics at the University of East Anglia (UEA) and on the PCAS form for Sociology and Economics at what was then Cambridgeshire College of Arts and Technology (CCAT). It is now Anglia Ruskin University.

I was offered an interview at UEA. However, the interview was a bit of a disaster, not least because I wasn't prepared for, what I now know in hindsight and also what I was told by my lecturers at Middlesex Polytechnic, were really difficult and unfair questions. Also, the interviewer seemed to become quite hostile after he asked me about my politics and I mentioned that I was a CPGB member. Anyway, my application was subsequently rejected. However, I was also offered an interview (or two interviews as it turned out – one for each subject) at CCAT. I was much more prepared for a grilling this time. However, the attitude of my interviewers couldn't have been more different. Stuart Wall, Course Leader for Economics, just chatted away about my interests and said that before I started in the Autumn, it would be a good idea to read some books that he recommended on maths for economists.

For Sociology, I was interviewed by Canadian Professor, Michelle Stanworth, author of the seminal text, *Gender and Schooling* (1983) that she was about to get published. Michelle said that her only concern was about my level of literacy skills, being as I'd been a manual worker all my working life. She asked to see some evidence of my written work. I said that I would send her some. I later sent her a copy of my project from the CIRTUS course at Middlesex Polytechnic and I also ambitiously wrote an essay on Marx's 1842 *Economic and Philosophic Manuscripts* (1988); well, why not go for it, I thought! I had a really delightful, long, hand-written letter back from Michelle saying that she had read both scripts that I had sent her and that she would be thrilled to accept me onto the Sociology course, starting in September.

During my year at Middlesex Polytechnic, Sue and I had been searching for a property in Lakenheath to buy at the same time as putting our three-bedroomed terraced house in Aveley on the market. We managed to sell our house and to buy a three bedroomed detached bungalow in Lakenheath and was still able to put quite a considerable sum into the bank to help see us through the three-year degree course. We moved to Lakenheath in June, 1982 after I had successfully completed the CIRTUS course.

From June until I started my degree course in the September of 1982 I needed to work to pay the bills and to try to get some money in the bank to help see us through the first year of study. I managed to get a job as a carpenter with the Lakenheath-based regional company, *Cocksedge and Sons*, for 12 weeks. It was National Working Rule Agreement pay and conditions, on the cards and there was an individual bonus scheme. I obviously didn't tell them that I planned to leave after 12 weeks.

Most of the time I worked on building a set of new public buildings in Bury-St-Edmunds. I was taken to the site every day in the back of a company van, along with several other workers. The bonus wasn't great, but I wasn't about to make any waves, being as I was only going to be with them for 12 weeks. I don't know if any of the other lads on the firm were trade unionists or not, but I avoided talking about trade unions or politics unless someone else mentioned them. Site conditions weren't too bad anyway, so I could suffer it for a short time. I worked with one lad as a pair for some of the time and we got on pretty well together.

As I said, I left in September 1982 to start my degree course at CCAT. Because I was a mature student supporting a wife and two children, the grant I got to study at CCAT was £4,200 a year. In addition to that, I claimed rate rebates, the children got free school meals and I signed on as unemployed during holiday periods. So, with a little bit of cash-in-hand for private carpentry jobs at the weekends, I didn't do too badly really. A local builder called Jimmy who just did small works like house extensions and so on, on his own account, in and around Lakenheath gave me lots of carpentry work to do during those three years and beyond, with no questions asked. Jimmy was also Chair of the Lakenheath Parish Council and with their blessing, he gave me a few jobs to do around the village, such as putting up notice boards. The job I am most proud of, though, is some rather ornate doors that I made and fitted to the entrance to the chapel in Lakenheath cemetery. Forty years later, they are still there, and I proudly point them out to people whenever I pass them.

I enjoyed the three-year study towards my BA Joint Honours in Economics and Sociology; more so the latter subject. Economics is a bit of a right-wing discipline with the main debates at the time being between monetarists and Keynesians. I only had a total of six lectures on Marxist economics in the whole three years; and they were given by an ill-informed Geography lecturer who was clearly hostile to his subject matter. Sociology, I found, was more questioning of the economic and social arrangements of capitalist societies, although some critics on the left regarded it as a 'bourgeois discipline'. Nevertheless, Marxist approaches did inform substantial parts of the course and it was at least more questioning of prevailing arrangements and discourses in society in general.

During my three years on the course, I made friends with other, mainly mature, students who thought similarly to me on most things. These group of friends included Martin, a CPGB member and ex-thatcher. We became known to the other students as 'the Marx brothers'. I also discovered that some of those who had come directly from independent schools weren't as 'bright' or as 'clued up' as we are sometimes led to believe. Indeed, some of them were totally clueless when it came to understanding how the majority of people in their own country lived and, indeed, struggled at times.

I was gobsmacked in one seminar on the economics of housing when one privately educated 18-year-old from a leafy London suburb said that he didn't realise that there were some people who didn't have anywhere to live! Honestly, you couldn't make it up. Some of these students from fee-paying schools had decided to come to CCAT because they weren't bright enough to get into Cambridge University but wanted to be able to tell people that they studied at Cambridge, which I thought was pretty pathetic!

The doors I made and fitted to the chapel in Lakenheath cemetery for Lakenheath Parish Council.

I did involve myself with the Student Union, which all students are automatically members of, but not to a great extent. I attended Student Union meetings that were held in the Mumford Theatre on campus and I campaigned for Andy, the left-wing Labour Party candidate in the election for the President. Unfortunately, Andy was beaten by the right-wing candidate. I also gave advice to the SU Executive on removal of asbestos from campus buildings and joined and took part in meetings of the Socialist Society. I was also invited by lecturers teaching on courses for civil engineers and surveyors to talk to students about the role of trade unions in the building industry; something I enjoyed, despite feeling a sense of hostility from some students.

The main focus of my activism, however, was still in UCATT. I discovered that the nearest branch to Lakenheath was in Thetford in Norfolk and so I effected a transfer to the branch from the Barking and Dagenham branch. I went along to my first branch meeting which was held in the Labour Club in Thetford and discovered that the Secretary, George, was there just to take subscriptions. Because of low attendance figures (not surprising in such a more rural area) he had abandoned trying to hold meetings some years earlier. Although a good trade unionist, George was retired and was looking for someone to take over from him as secretary. He asked me if I would take over because nobody else had come forward. I agreed.

The first thing that I did was to write to all the members telling them that I intended to start holding meetings again and inviting them to come along to discuss any issues that they had. At the first meeting, there were about 10 members who attended, five of whom worked at *Omar Park and Leisure Homes* in nearby Brandon making mobile homes. Colin was their union rep. at the plant and he had persuaded the others to come along with him. Ken, a bricklayer who worked for various companies around the area, was already chairman of the branch. He was a quiet bloke but efficient and committed to the union. After that we got about five or six to subsequent meetings; just about enough to be quorate, to hold meaningful discussions and to make decisions.

In October 1982, with unemployment still rising and with one in five workers, especially building workers, experiencing unemployment during that year, the London Regional Council of UCATT organised a coach to take members to a protest rally of all workers that was due to take place outside the Tory Party conference in Brighton. I decided to miss lectures and go. On the outskirts of Brighton, the police were stopping all coaches going to the rally, boarding them and questioning 'the person in charge' on each coach. George O'Driscoll, the UCATT Regional Chairman, announced himself as the person in charge on our coach. As soon as the police heard his Irish accent, they made all of us get off the coach while they searched it. This was two years before the IRA bombed the hotel where most of the delegates for the Tory Party Conference were staying.

Anyway, after the protest rally, John Barlow, a Labour Party member and unemployed bricklayer, and myself decided to find a decent pub for some lunch. As we were walking through the back streets of Brighton we spotted the notorious Thatcherite Tory MP for Southend-On-Sea, Teddy Taylor, walking along the other side of the road. John said to me: 'I'm going to have him!' I said 'Be careful, John. Don't do anything silly.' We crossed the road and John politely asked him what he was going to do about the unacceptable level of unemployment of building workers, especially as the *London Brick Company* were stockpiling bricks, thousands were homeless, yet building workers like him couldn't get jobs. He was very cool and articulate, given his personal situation. Taylor replied: 'Well, we've got to get the economy right first' to which John retorted: 'So, while you're getting the economy right, I've got to sit on my backside at home doing nothing, have I?' Taylor made an excuse that he was late for the conference and had to dash. He scurried away, clearly nonplussed.

We went on to find a good pub where we had some lunch and a few pints. On the coach going back to London we realised that we had left the UCATT London Regional banner that the pair of us had been put in charge of, in the corner of the bar. Luckily, the landlord was sympathetic to trade unions, wrapped it up and sent it back to the London Regional Office and didn't charge us anything for doing so.

In 1983, with unemployment still a major problem, between April and June of that year, a second 'People's March for Jobs' took place from Glasgow to London. The march came through Cambridge and we organised, through the Student Union, to meet and greet them at a community centre on the outskirts of the city, where an outdoor rally with speeches was held. Gary, who was the labourers' shop steward that I had worked with several years earlier on the GLC site at Harold Hill, was one of the marchers and we had a good chat about what we'd both been doing since. The march went on to London where 20,000 people attended a rally in Hyde Park to mark the end of the march. The rally was addressed by Labour leader Michael Foot and the general secretary of the TUC, Len Murray.

As Secretary of the UCATT Thetford branch, I also received a letter from Thetford Trades Council in late 1983 inviting us to send a delegate. The branch elected me to represent us at the Trades Council which was held in the same building. Not long afterwards, the most bitter industrial dispute in recent British history, the national miners' strike over pit closures, started in March, 1984 and the Thetford Trades Council played its part in supporting striking miners. We started by going round with buckets collecting money for the strikers on Saturdays, market day, in Thetford. Two of our number got arrested for 'begging' because the miners were not a registered charity. They were held all day at Thetford Police Station and then released at the end of the day with no charges brought. They were not given the money back that they had collected, being told by laughing officers that it would be donated to the 'Police Benevolent Fund'. Given that the police were playing a key role in the strike, attacking striking miners and acting as Thatcher's private army, they were taking the p**s really.

After that, the local vicar who was sympathetic to the miners' cause, gave us permission to set up a stall on church ground by the side of the market square to do collections, saying to us that the police had no jurisdiction to prevent us from doing so there. We mainly asked for food donations from the public. There was a supermarket just round the corner and it was from there that most of the donations came from the public. We did get some hostility and some abuse thrown at us, but that wasn't unexpected in such a Tory area and it was like water off a duck's back to us anyway. On the other hand, we were delighted with the generosity and level of support shown by many of the public. On one occasion we were astounded when a young girl who couldn't have been more than about 12-years-old, brought along a whole supermarket trolly full of food, saying that her dad was just round the corner in the supermarket and had asked her to bring it along to us, but he wanted to remain anonymous.

In 1984 I was elected as Chairman of the Thetford Trades Council. As a Trades Council, we adopted Harworth Colliery in Nottinghamshire to support during the strike. Miners in other parts of the country considered Nottinghamshire miners as 'rats' and 'scabs' because the majority of miners in the Nottinghamshire coalfields didn't support the strike. However, we chose a Nottinghamshire pit to support because those minority of lads who did come out in support of the strike in those coalfields had a much tougher time of it than those in places like South Wales, Yorkshire, Scotland or Kent. They had little or no support from their local communities and, indeed, were treated like pariahs by local people.

In visits to Harworth to take food parcels and to support the miners who were on strike on picket lines, I witnessed some of the police brutality towards pickets, especially from the Metropolitan Police officers who had been bussed there as part of 'Thatcher's army'. When they were being driven away from the picket lines in the evening in their buses, I also witnessed some of these officers waving £10 notes out of the windows at miners to signify that they were getting loads of money from overtime whilst miners were starving. I've always found it difficult to empathise with any police officer since, however progressive they might appear to be or might say that they are.

As a Students' Union at CCAT, we also invited some Yorkshire miners to come and speak to a meeting of all the students at the college. A considerable sum of money was raised to support the miners, despite the fact that most students were living on very meagre grants and could hardly afford to contribute to their cause. Sadly, as most people know, the strike ended in defeat after a year in March, 1985. With the whole of the establishment, including the capitalist class, the government, the judiciary, the police and almost all of the capitalist media against them, it was always going to be difficult for the miners to win.

During my time as a student, I also became more involved in the machinery of government of the Eastern Region of UCATT. In 1984, I stood for and was elected as a delegate to the biennial national delegate conference which was held in Bournemouth. Sue and the children came with me and we stayed with our friends Jackie and Alan at their place in Southbourne. It was a holiday for Sue and the boys whilst I was in the conference hall every day.

As a branch secretary, I also attended and spoke at the Eastern Region conference of UCATT on putting a greater emphasis on servicing existing members rather than simply trying to recruit more; the latter strategy had simply been having a debilitating effect on the organisation as it had led to somewhat of a 'revolving door' effect, or what I described as 'there's a hole in my bucket' effect where the faster we filled the bucket with new members the bigger the hole got in the bottom. This speech seemed to go down really well and the motion was adopted overwhelmingly.

I was invited to attend meetings of the Eastern Region 'broad left' grouping of UCATT which held its meetings in Stevenage. The broad left grouping had been set up mainly to campaign for more militant UCATT policies both regionally and nationally and to support left candidates in union elections. It was composed of CPGB members, left Labour Party members, Militant and others on the left from other minor parties and none. The heartening thing about it was that there was never a trace of sectarianism in the group and in supporting particular candidates in elections nobody ever asked what their political affiliations were. It is that kind of solidarity that I've always believed is what we should be aiming for in the trade union and labour movement. Ideological differences over the Russian revolution and whether or not the Labour Party could be a truly revolutionary party, for example, always seemed to me to be barriers to making progress in the labour and trade union movement.

One of the major obstacles to progress, however, was that we knew that some branches who had right-wing secretaries were fiddling the elections to try to get their preferred candidates elected to posts. Votes were supposed to take place for candidates at branch meetings after the election addresses of all the candidates had been read out. We had very strong suspicions that some right-wing secretaries were not only not doing this but also, that they were simply recording their whole membership as voting for the secretaries' preferred candidates.

So, at election times, as a 'broad left' grouping, we divided up all the right-wing led branches in the region between us and made sure that every branch that was under suspicion was visited. Under UCATT rules we were entitled to do this as long as we were just there as observers. We could not take part in or vote at those branch meetings. I visited a number of such branches and was usually given a hostile reception with questions such as 'what are you doing here?' My stock response was that I just happened to be in the area and just wanted to bring fraternal greetings to the branch. Anyway, after that campaign, unsurprisingly, more left candidates started getting elected to union positions.

Indeed, I was asked by the broad left grouping to stand as a broad left candidate for the Eastern Regional Council myself. It was against a strong field, as most Regional Council elections were in those days. So, I had to campaign vigorously and write a powerful election address. I think my speech at the Eastern Regional Conference had helped secure the support of the non-aligned membership as well and I was duly elected in 1985. At the first meeting of the Eastern Regional Council of UCATT, I was elected as chairman, though I told the other delegates that I preferred the non-sexist term 'president'.

The full-time Eastern Regional Secretary was none other than CPGB member, Dave Hardie, who had worked for *Laings* as a carpenter on the Littlebrook site when I had been there. He had been elected as a full-time official a few years earlier and then had risen to the post of Regional Secretary. One of the things that became apparent at the first few meetings was that we would spend nearly all day going through 'matters arising' from the last meeting as few of those issues had been resolved. We wouldn't start on new business until about five o'clock in the afternoon. Dave's secretary, Jane, took the minutes and I moved that we should delegate each problem to a specific person in the minutes, either a lay person or a full-time official, who would then be charged with reporting back at the next meeting on what action they had taken over those issues. It didn't entirely resolve the situation but many issues started to get resolved more quickly and we were able to move on to other issues much earlier in the day.

There were also strains between the Regional Council members and the full-time organisers that had been going on for some time. We decided to organise a weekend away for Regional Council members and full-time officials at Great Yarmouth where we thrashed out our differences as well as socialising in the evenings. Sue and the kids came with me, so they got a weekend away at the seaside where they could do the usual things that holidaymakers did during the day whilst I was in conference and Sue and I could socialise with the other delegates and their partners in the evening at the hotel whilst the kids slept.

In 1985 I was also elected as a delegate from the Thetford Trades Council to the Norfolk Association of Trades Councils. I was then elected by the Norfolk Association of Trades Councils as a delegate to the South-East Region of the TUC (SERTUC). I became an active member of SERTUC and was elected to serve on its Education sub-committee. By this time I was heavily involved in labour movement activities in the Eastern region.

One of the annual highlights of the calendar in this region has been the *Burston Strike School Rally* which has been held at the small village of Burston in Norfolk since 1984. The rally, held on the village green on the first Sunday in September, commemorates the longest strike in history. Teachers and socialists Annie and Tom Higdon were sacked on trumped-up charges in 1914 and all the pupils walked out in support of them. The local squirarchy were offended by their presence in the village and the care that they showed for the children in their school. They decided to get rid of them after Tom and a number of his supporters had got themselves elected as Labour members to the local council.

The strike lasted for 25 years. The annual march around the village and rally on the village green is attended by about 5000 trade unionists each year who hear bands, poets and speakers as well as getting the chance to visit the 50 to 100 labour movement stalls. I have attended the rally almost every year since it started and have heard such wonderful speakers as Dennis Skinner, Tony Benn and Jeremy Corbyn. It is so uplifting to meet so many like-minded, progressive people in an area that is, on the surface, deeply conservative and Conservative!

I graduated from CCAT in 1985 with an upper-second class joint honours degree in Sociology and Economics. At the time students were consulted on who they wanted to present their degrees at the graduation ceremony. As a last act of defiance over the outcome of the miners' strike, Martin and I campaigned amongst our fellow students to ask that Mick McGahey, the Scottish miners' leader, be asked to do the honours. Despite him getting more votes than anyone else, the college refused to ask him. A historian, unknown even to those studying history, was chosen instead.

I had been applying for graduate jobs for some time. Because I was an economics undergraduate, at the college's jobs fair, I had been offered a post as a trainee broker but, given my political beliefs, I was never going to go down that route! After graduating, I did get shortlisted for two jobs that I had applied for during the next couple of months though. One was working for Peterborough City Council promoting and supporting worker cooperatives. The second one was working as an ambassador for the United Nations Association, promoting the cause of international cooperation. For both posts I got down to the last two but I was unsuccessful in both cases. I did get some work as a visiting lecturer/sessional tutor for the Cambridge branch of the Workers Educational Association, but I really needed a full-time job.

So, in June 1985, I went back on the tools working as a maintenance carpenter for Breckland District Council based in Thetford. Again, it was a closed-shop and every worker in the yard was a member of the appropriate union. Every trade was also represented by a shop steward. Most of the half a dozen carpenters were members of the Thetford branch of UCATT, of which I was Branch Secretary of course. We worked in pairs with each pair getting a council van between them. I worked with Richard, a quiet local lad who was younger than me, single and who was a regular attender at branch meetings. We got on well together, even though the conversation was rather limited at times. It was National Working Rule Agreement wages and conditions and there was an individual bonus scheme in operation. The job suited me for the time being until something better came along.

I was only there for three months when I saw an advertisement for exactly the same position, council-employed maintenance carpenter, working for Forest Heath District Council based in Mildenhall. Mildenhall was much closer to home, so I applied and got the job. The wages and conditions were the same with an individual bonus scheme and, again, it was a closed shop. On this job I was given a council van of my own and asked to service the town of Brandon on my own. When I'd cleared up all the backlog of jobs in Brandon, I was given other ones in other villages, including my own in Lakenheath. I also helped out some of the other lads to clear up the outstanding jobs in the town of Mildenhall.

Chapter 9

From wood butcher to academic!

I hadn't been at Forest Heath District Council very long when I received a phone call one evening from a lecturer called David Slade at the West Suffolk College in Bury-St-Edmunds; the nearest FE College to where I lived. It was a call that was about to change my working life. He said that the College were advertising a General Certificate of Education (GCE) 'O' Level one-year intensive course in Sociology one evening a week and that they didn't have a lecturer to teach it. He went on to say that someone (he didn't say who and to this day I still don't know who it was!) had given him my name and told him that I had a degree in Sociology, so, would I be interested in teaching it?

At first, I said that I hadn't taught before and was dubious about my ability to do so. He reassured me that, as I had a degree in the subject, I shouldn't find it too difficult to teach GCE 'O' Level. Anyway, I was still sceptical, but I agreed to go for an interview with him at the College. At the interview I was told that 27 students had already been recruited for the course, it was due to start in two weeks' time and that they were desperate to find someone to teach it. I thought that I must be mad, but I agreed to give it a go. I was given the syllabus and had just two weeks to prepare some teaching materials and to order library resources for students.

When I turned up for the first class there were, indeed, 27 students who were all as keen as mustard, mature adults. At first, I was very nervous, but, although in hindsight I made many mistakes, the course went well and many of them got good grades at the end of the year. It was the last year of GCE 'O' Levels before they were amalgamated with the Certificate of Secondary Education (CSE) examinations to become General Certificate of

Secondary Education (GCSE). After attending sessions with a full-time lecturer, John Garbutt, on how the new GCSEs would work, I was asked to teach the new GCSE in Sociology, again as a one-year intensive evening class, in the following academic year.

There was also a one-year intensive 'A' Level in Sociology running during the day in which mature students had 10 hours tuition a week. I was also offered six of those hours a week. At first, I said that I couldn't do it as I had a full-time job that I couldn't afford to give up. Then I saw that the TUC Education Department at Peterborough Regional College were looking for a part-time tutor on a course-by-course basis for their outreach programme of union reps. courses across East Anglia; right up my street and something that I thought I'd love to do! I thought I could combine this with my GCSE and 'A' Level teaching at West Suffolk College. I applied for and was appointed to tutor courses at Peterborough Regional College, Suffolk College and Lowestoft College. So, I accepted the 'A' Level Sociology daytime teaching as well as the GCSE Sociology teaching at West Suffolk College.

I also got a bit of teaching with the Open College. I packed up my maintenance carpentry job at Forest Heath District Council as I embarked on an academic career. However, I still had to supplement my income with the odd carpentry jobs for the local builder Jimmy who I mentioned earlier. On Saturday mornings, I started attending the Thetford Adult Education Centre for tutor training with a guy called Paul and I submitted proposals to teach evening classes in Thetford. Thetford is in Norfolk, but it is about equidistant to Bury-St-Edmunds from where I live. I did teach GCSE Sociology at the Charles Burrell School as an adult class in Thetford, but when Paul, who was also promoting other courses in South Norfolk, left, the work dried up.

As a pre-requisite for teaching the TUC union reps. courses, I went on a residential tutor training course for a week at the new TUC Education Centre which was housed in the old Hornsey College of Art building in Crouch End. The facilities were first class and the training in student-centred teaching was second to none. I absolutely loved the mural that adorned one of the walls there that was painted by Paul Butler and Desmond Rochford depicting the history of the labour movement, starting with the machine breaking Luddites and ending with the big strikes by printers, dockers and miners. Years later it was considered 'inappropriate' by the 'New Labour' commercialism that had taken over much of the labour movement and was, criminally in my opinion, painted over, despite calls by many activists to preserve it.

Obviously, all the students on the course were committed trade unionists and in the evenings one or two students brought their guitars along to the bar and we had a really good time drinking and singing inspiring songs such as *Solidarity Forever, The Internationale, McAlpine's Fusiliers* and the Peggy Seeger, feminist anthem *I'm Gonna Be an Engineer*. Those nights are among my fondest memories of labour movement solidarity.

I really enjoyed the next three years, especially teaching the union reps. courses for the TUC. Before each course I would meet the head of trade union courses at Peterborough Regional College at a roadside café about halfway between my home in Lakenheath and the college in Peterborough so that he could transfer all the course materials from the boot of his car to mine and to discuss forthcoming courses and how I was going to tutor them. I tried to get TUC union reps. courses going at West Suffolk College in Bury St. Edmunds, but, due to financial constraints, without success. In 1989 I once again attended a residential course at the TUC Education Centre in Crouch End for teaching the Stage 1 Health and Safety course which I only taught once because my career was about to take another turn.

I had been teaching GCSE and 'A' Level Sociology as well as other courses such as Communications Studies to construction apprentices at West Suffolk College on an hourly paid basis for three years when a new, rather assertive, Head of Faculty took over for Humanities and Social Sciences. She quickly recognised the value of the work that I was doing and asked me why I wasn't a permanent, full-time member of staff. I replied that I simply hadn't been offered a job. She said that wasn't right, marched me over to the Principal's office and demanded that I be made permanent immediately. The principal was rather taken aback but promised to advertise a post for a Lecturer in Communications and Sociology, teaching everything that I had been teaching and that I could apply for it.

The job description was clearly written with me in mind, but the Board of Governors insisted that all new posts had to be advertised externally. Although most of what I had been teaching was Sociology, it was explained to me that the post had to be advertised as 'Communications and Sociology' with the implication that Communication Studies was the main focus of the appointment because the Board was comprised predominantly of local businessmen who were, not surprisingly, very 'conservative' and that sociology was regarded as a left-wing discipline. Board members would be on the interview panel.

Indeed, at interview, I was asked if I didn't think that teaching sociology to young people might indoctrinate them into left-wing views. My answer was that education should be about opening young peoples' minds to questioning everything about the society that they live in rather than closing their minds, which is what indoctrination is. That seemed to satisfy the Board. Anyway, there were three applicants including myself but, not surprisingly, I was appointed to the post. Initially, it was only for one year and I would have to apply the following year for a continuation of the appointment. I was delighted to get my first appointment as a full-time lecturer.

By this time, I was drowning in activist commitments. I was Thetford Branch Secretary of UCATT, UCATT Eastern Regional Council Chairman, UCATT Conference delegate, UCATT TUC delegate, Thetford Trades Council chairman, Norfolk County Association of Trades Councils delegate, TUC Eastern Region delegate and TUC Eastern Region Education Sub-Committee member. I was also active in the Anti-Apartheid Movement, the Cuba Solidarity Campaign and the National Secular Society. In addition, I was heavily involved in the CPGB, being chair of the Thetford branch and organising events on a regular basis.

It was all having an effect on my mental health, on my marriage and I was missing so much of seeing my children grow up because I was hardly ever at home. I was really feeling the strain. I just had to take a break from it all. Luckily, events unfolded that allowed me to do just that. It was a closed shop at the college and every lecturer was a member of the National Association of Teachers in Further and Higher Education (NATFHE). As a new starter as a lecturer at the college, I was approached by the Branch Secretary to join. I explained that I needed to transfer from UCATT, but that I had to 'put things in order' with my commitments to UCATT before I could transfer. This was acceptable to him.

I resigned from the Eastern Regional Council of UCATT but stayed to help the broad left support another very able candidate for election. At the next UCATT branch meeting,

Colin, the union rep. at *Omar Park and Leisure Homes* agreed to take over as branch secretary and I spent an evening with him showing him the ropes. This also meant that I had to tender my resignation with the Thetford Trades Council. Don, a New Communist Party (NCP) member and very able comrade, took over. This meant that my roles as delegate to the County Association of Trades Councils, SERTUC and the SERTUC Education Sub-Committee were also terminated.

In the late 80s the CPGB was also splitting up between what were unhelpfully described as 'Tankies' and 'Eurocommunists'. I had my differences with both groups. On the one hand, I had always had problems with the strict application of the principle of 'democratic centralism' whilst on the other hand I was no fan of the more 'liberal' culturalism of the Eurocommunist faction. The former group established the Communist Party of Britain in 1988, whilst the latter group disbanded the CPGB and established the so-called Democratic Left in 1991. So, after 17 years in the CPGB, I found I no longer had a political home.

I scaled down my involvement in the Anti-Apartheid Movement, now Action for Southern Africa (ACSA), the Cuba Solidarity Campaign and the National Secular Society, although I continued with my membership of those organisations. For the first time in many years, I felt as if a huge burden had been lifted off my shoulders. My mental health improved as did my marriage and my relationship with my children. I vowed never to get so involved as an activist ever again, although I also vowed to 'step up to the plate' in emergencies or when I had to with regard to labour movement activities.

At the end of that first year as a full-time lecturer, I was offered another one-year contract and again the following year. However, the college couldn't keep doing that because 'the Silver Book', which was the set of agreements between the unions and colleges, stipulated that colleges could only do this with a lecturer for a maximum of three consecutive years. So, when the college tried to do it again, my union rep., John Garbutt, insisted that the college had to make it permanent, which they did.

Little did I know at the time that it wouldn't be long before I was required to 'step up to the plate' once again. Until that time the so-called 'Silver Book' that I just referred to set limits on the working and teaching year, the length of terms and class contact hours with additional pay for hours above the minimum and stipulated at least six weeks' continuous summer holiday amongst a plethora of other working conditions. It was a large and comprehensive agreement that was a testament to the hard bargaining that NATFHE had put in over many years and indicative of what a strong union could get for its members in those days. However, things were about to change. The Silver Book was like a running sore to the Thatcherites. Firstly, in 1990, legislation was enacted to outlaw the closed shop which was ultimately to weaken NATFHE, as it did all other trade unions.

Previously, in 1985, new trade union laws had required that General Secretaries had to be re-elected every five years by a vote of the membership. This was designed by the Thatcher government to try to get rid of left-wing leaders, but in NATFHE it had quite the opposite effect. In 1990 Peter Dawson, an experienced trade union official, was defeated in the NATFHE leadership contest by the ultra-left supported candidate, Geoff Woolf. At the same time, Further Education Colleges were also taken out of local authority control, and pay negotiations were undertaken by a new national body run by a former trade union official, Roger Ward. Ward was to become NATFHE's nemesis. Ward and the college bosses set to work to try to destroy NATFHE. They drafted a new contract, designed to replace the Silver Book, to place lecturers under their employers' collective thumbs, and decreed that only lecturers who signed it would get a pay rise.

In what to my mind was a disastrous move, the NATFHE leadership reacted by breaking off negotiations with the employers' organisation and instructing Branch Secretaries to negotiate with their individual colleges to get the best deals that they could get at local level. It was a move designed to create chaos in the sector and to force individual colleges to get mired in negotiations and disputes that many of them were reluctant to do. However, what it did mean in practice was that members of weaker branches were being sacrificed and was the opposite of the 'unity is strength' principle that national bargaining provided. There were the odd strike days across the country, including at West Suffolk College, but it was difficult to get lecturers, who had got used to a comfortable co-existence with their employers for many years, to take sustained industrial action.

At West Suffolk College the Branch Secretary had worked at the college for many years and was nearing retirement. He felt that it wouldn't be right for him to engage in negotiations with the college, not least because he had no experience of negotiating terms and conditions of employment with employers, but also, because of his imminent retirement, it wouldn't be fair to negotiate terms and conditions that he wouldn't have to work under. A branch meeting was called and several members suggested that, as I had experience of negotiating with employers, I should take over as Branch Secretary. I said that I may have experience of negotiating with employers, but that it was in an entirely different sector of the economy.

However, I wasn't about to shirk my responsibilities, so I suggested that I would do it, but only if I had representatives from other departments in the college to help me. This was agreed and it was also agreed by the college management. Subsequently, Gary was elected from the Hospitality Department, Mark was elected from Hairdressing and Penny was elected from Business Studies. I asked them all to go on TUC union reps. courses and sought and got permission from the College Principal for them to do so. As for Gary, Mark and Penny, they were only too happy to do the training and we ended up being a good team. I was to be the lead negotiator, but it was a bit like the blind leading the blind to be honest.

The Principal, a bumptious and righteous individual also retired and lengthy negotiations then took place over supposed new contracts to enable all lecturers to receive the nationally agreed, or rather imposed, pay rise with his replacement, Nick, who was promoted from Deputy Principal. Nick was much more amenable to compromise. He was a thoughtful and intelligent man who valued trade union involvement in college affairs. He was a bit 'New Labourish', but at least it was possible to have meaningful discussions with him. In fact, I was the first one that Nick came to see the morning after the General Election in 1997 to shake my hand on the election of a Labour government.

At negotiations, Nick would also bring along the college's accountant, David, with him. David was part of the management team and he would have a big say in what was agreed. Indeed, at times we would be negotiating with David alone when the Principal had other business to attend to. David would later get approval from Nick on what had been agreed. Meetings rarely took place with all four of us union reps. present either, because there was usually one or more of us that couldn't attend due to teaching commitments.

The tone of the meetings that was set by Nick and David was that they really wanted to give us the pay rise, but that they had to satisfy the board that what was agreed was genuinely a new contract that departed from 'the Silver Book' and that we had conceded on holiday entitlements and other, what they described as, 'restrictive practices'; what trade unionists always describe as 'protective practices.' In the end we agreed to a fairly minimalist agreement with very few concessions apart from the stipulation that at least six weeks' continuous summer holiday would be reduced to four. I must stress that this wasn't a cut of two weeks' holiday.

There were about 12 weeks in the summer when little or no teaching took place, but there were other activities that lecturers were presumed to be doing such as exam invigilation, meetings, conferences, open days, preparing teaching materials for the following year and so on. The Silver Book had simply stipulated that during this period lecturers should be allowed to take six continuous weeks of their holidays without interruption. The college wanted this reduced to four. In the end we came to an agreement, but crucially, we had inserted in the small print that where the agreement was silent on any issue, reference would be made back to the Silver Book.

We consulted the full-time NATFHE official about what we had agreed because he was au fait with agreements that had been made at other colleges up and down the country. He assured us that this was probably the sixth best agreement that he had seen to date and that by that time most branches had made agreements with their respective colleges. We put this agreement to a mass meeting of lecturers without recommendation. Virtually every lecturer in the college was at that meeting; the first time I'd seen that happen. Everyone was in favour of accepting the deal except Roger, a lecturer from the Engineering Department. Roger had been an active trade unionist all his working life, principally in the Amalgamated Engineering Union (AEU). He argued that we should never trade hard-won conditions of employment for more money. I must admit that I had some sympathy with Roger's arguments, and I wasn't entirely happy about it myself, but he was a lone voice and the deal was agreed. Sadly, Roger was killed in a freak accident when he was hit by a runaway lorry wheel after a road collision shortly after this.

After that, there were some 'skirmishes' every year over pay and conditions negotiations and the odd days strikes, but by and large, relations were pretty good with the college. Despite the legislation outlawing the closed shop, NATFHE membership remained either at or close to 100 per cent. What helped this was that when new lecturers were taken on it was part of their interviews to mention that their pay and conditions were negotiated with NATFHE and that they would be 'invited' to join if they were appointed. On their first day, all new lecturers would have a day full of induction activities, part of which I, Gary, Mark or Penny would be invited along to talk about the work of NATFHE and to sign up new lecturers. This was all encouraged by the Principal, Nick.

So, for the next few years I concentrated on building my career and building up my portfolio. The college had agreed to give lecturers time off and pay course fees for any relevant training that they wanted to do. I had already successfully completed the City and Guilds Teacher Training Course that was taught in-house. Interestingly, Nick, the College Principal taught a few sessions on this course. He said that he thought it was important that he 'kept his hand in' and continued to experience 'the chalkface', if only minimally, if he was going to be dealing with the problems that lecturers faced. After successfully completing the City and Guilds, I studied for another teaching qualification, the Certificate in Education (FE) with what was then Anglia Polytechnic. I successfully completed the course in 1992.

I was made Head of Sociology and 'A' Level Course Director for a 22 subject, college-wide programme for 16-18-year-olds and a five subject one-year intensive 'A' Level course for adults. Thanks to Dave Kent, Head of History in my department, we also developed an Access to Higher Education course in Humanities and Social Sciences which was validated by the Cambridge Access Validating Agency; an organisation that I was later to become a board member of. As the college wanted to develop undergraduate teaching, several of us were encouraged to apply for postgraduate courses that the college would pay for and give us time off to pursue. I studied part-time for a Master's degree in sociology at the prestigious Essex University near Colchester where I graduated in 1995.

During my time there, West Suffolk College became part of the Anglia Polytechnic University's Regional Student Scheme which taught undergraduate courses at colleges throughout East Anglia. At West Suffolk College I became Sociology Lead on the BA (Hons) Combined Humanities/Social Sciences Course and module leader for six modules. As a consequence, I was made an Honorary Lecturer of Anglia Polytechnic University. I also started teaching on the Certificate in Education (FE) that only a few years earlier I had been a student on. In 1988, I also started teaching on a new BA (Ed) teacher training course.

By this time, I had had a few articles published in *Social Science Teacher* and *Sociology Review* and I had presented papers at several annual conferences of the *Association of Teachers of Social Science* (ATSS). I thought that I was ready for teaching in a Higher Education institution. I applied for a job as a Senior Lecturer in Sociology at Leeds Metropolitan University in 1989. I was interviewed and got the job. The Principal at West Suffolk College was one of the first to come and congratulate me on my appointment and said that I fully deserved it for the hard work that I had put in.

The lecturing staff at Leeds Metropolitan University were highly unionised. It is difficult to say whether or not it was 100 per cent unionised because of the number of Faculties spread over three sites, but there were very able branch officers and well-attended branch meetings. By this time, both our kids had left home, so Sue and I rented a cottage in Morley on the outskirts of Leeds for six months while we looked for a one-bedroom place to buy on a 15-year mortgage. We had paid the mortgage up on our home in Lakenheath some years earlier. Eventually, we bought a one-bedroom maisonette in Morley, which is near Leeds, where we stayed during the week. Every other week during term times we came home to our bungalow in Lakenheath and we stayed there for most of the holidays. Sue was a bookkeeper and she could take her work anywhere with her.

At the university, the Head of Department suggested to me that I undertake a PhD and that the department would pay my fees and give me time off my duties in which to do the research. I already had a research idea and so I applied with the university graduate research department and managed to find Jonathan Long, a professor, who was willing to supervise me, as well as Ron Brown, a secondary supervisor. A full-time PhD usually takes three years, but as I was doing it part-time, it was expected that I would complete it in six years, especially as I had to complete a Postgraduate Certificate in Research Methodology first.

However, not long after I had registered for the degree, I found that not only were my duties not slimmed down by my Head of Department but also that I had other duties added to those that I already had. Firstly, I was asked to be Admissions Tutor for the Sociology undergraduate course. This was more substantial than it sounds. I had to sort through more than 400 UCAS applications every year (by this time UCCA and PCAS had amalgamated) which meant reading through all applicants' qualifications, references and statements, rejecting some, giving unconditional offers to some, asking some to come for interviews which I had to conduct in order to whittle down the 400 applicants to 40 places. It also meant organising and staffing open days to tell aspiring applicants about the university and the course, as well as dealing with clearing in the weeks after the 'A' Level results confirmed that some who had been offered conditional places hadn't achieved the grades that they had been asked to get as well as new applicants through clearing who didn't have places elsewhere. Altogether, it was a huge undertaking.

If that wasn't enough, I then had the course leadership foisted onto me because Mike, who had been doing the job, fell ill and was unable to continue doing it. This might seem like an honour but it involved organising and coordinating the activities, lectures, seminars and tutorials, of several Senior Lecturers and modules in three different departments each year; again, a huge undertaking on its own when one considers that this was all on top of my own portfolio of teaching and learning. As budgets and teaching staff were cut, I not only didn't get a reduction in teaching time but also I saw my teaching increase. I got absolutely no help from the Head of Department who had promised so much.

I decided that, using the university's grievance procedure, I was going to take out a grievance against the Head of Department and the Dean who was equally unsympathetic. However, I wasn't the only Senior Lecturer in the department who was being treated in this way. A colleague, Steve, suggested that if we all took out grievances individually, we could be picked off one-by-one. With the support of the NATFHE branch we set up a sub-group of all the Senior Lecturers in our department and submitted a group grievance. Meetings took place with the Head of Department and the Dean where they took a hard line approach. Nevertheless, the writing was on the wall for them for their intransigent attitude and they were both eventually replaced. Mary, an ex-sociology lecturer and much more supportive colleague was appointed as Dean and Steve, a Quaker and really caring bloke, was appointed as the Head of Department. Although things were better, it still took me seven years to complete my PhD.

However, in 2005, after seven years, I was getting tired of travelling back and forth to Leeds and so I was looking for a post closer to my home in Lakenheath. I saw an advertisement for a Senior Lecturer in Sociology and Criminology at the Bedford campus of De Montfort University. I realised that the post was to replace Paul Manning, a sociologist who I had known for a number of years through conferences and guest lectures, who was moving on. I thought that Bedford was within daily traveling distance of my home in Lakenheath, so I applied for the post. I was interviewed for the job along with two other shortlisted candidates and I was appointed.

However, I hadn't been there long when I suffered a stroke. I was totally paralysed at first, but due to the swift and excellent care I received, firstly from the paramedics who attended the scene, my home, and then from the medical staff at Addenbrookes Hospital in Cambridge, I made almost a complete recovery over the course of just one week. I was off work for a further few weeks, after which I had to seriously evaluate my activity, including my workplace trade union activity. Interestingly, two of the three main NATFHE branch officers were sociologists working in the same department as me and they were the two Senior Lecturers who were on the panel that had interviewed me. Bob and Phil were excellent union reps. and I had no need to become more involved in trade union activity, other than giving them my full support.

I was assured at the interview with senior management that the campus had a very bright future as part of the Leicester-based De Montfort University. I hadn't been there long, though, when a staff meeting of the whole campus was convened to tell us that De Montfort University was selling off the campus to the University of Luton and the university would be renamed the University of Bedfordshire. Although, by this time there wasn't 100 per cent union membership on the Bedford campus, NATFHE had a pretty strong presence, with only the Sports Studies Department having few members. Indeed, the Sports Studies department had a culture of hostility to trade unions, as was to become evident later on. University of Luton staff were much less well-organised. Between 2005 and 2007 NATFHE merged with the Association of University Teachers (AUT) to form the University and College Union (UCU).

Until the merger was finally completed, AUT and NATFHE members in Higher Education, including myself, had been involved in ongoing 'action short of a strike'. This included boycotting setting and marking exams, and 'mark and park' where we would mark coursework but we would not release marks to students or the exam boards. This action was continued by UCU members, including myself, after the merger. We were taking action over issues of pay, and the gap that had grown over the previous 20 to 30 years between our salaries and that of other similarly qualified public-sector professionals. The 'New Labour' Prime Minister, Tony Blair, had promised that a significant percentage of new investment released for universities would be put towards lecturers' pay. Not surprisingly, this did not happen. AUT and NATFHE rejected an offer of 12.6 per cent over three years and a further offer of 13.12 per cent over three years.

Concerns grew that students would not be able to graduate in 2006. The National Union of Students' (NUS) leadership supported our action and, although the matter was raised at various meetings, NUS support for us was never successfully challenged. In response to feedback from a group of students' unions, NUS advised AUT/NATFHE (UCU) that their support for action could not be indefinite and was wholly dependent on seeking a fast resolution. Many Students' Unions from around the country went further and openly condemned the action taken by the lecturers as holding the students to ransom; a sad indictment of how students had been depoliticised and individualised since those heady days of the 1960s when university students were in the forefront of solidarity with workers' actions. Although they were only a small minority at my campus, I had to remind a handful of my students who took this attitude that they might need our support in the none too distant future; a prescient observation on my part as it subsequently turned out.

To support the industrial action the new union, on its very first day of existence, organised a 'day of solidarity' by its Higher Education members. This included a demonstration in London which ended with a lobby at the headquarters of the employers' body, the Universities and Colleges Employers' Association (UCEA) which I went to. There were also strike days which I enthusiastically took part in, doing more than my fair share of picket duty. Two things stand out about those days on the picket line. Firstly, the Dean of our Faculty who was sympathetic to our cause, used to bring tea and biscuits out onto the picket line for us. How civilised! That would never have happened on a building site. Secondly, some non-union members of staff, mostly from the Sports Studies Department, drove through picket lines, often at speed, endangering the lives of pickets like myself, often making rude gestures and comments as they sped away. Not surprisingly, I never heard of any of these scabs refusing to accept the deal that was finally negotiated by UCU with the employers.

Following further talks between UCU and UCEA, sponsored by the TUC and ACAS, UCU agreed to ballot its members on the 13.1% offer (with an increase of around 15% for lower paid members of non-academic university staff) over three years, with the important proviso that any money docked from striking lecturers would be repaid and that an independent review would consider the mechanisms for future negotiations and the scope of funding available to universities for future pay settlements. The pay increase was phased over the three years, with the final year's figure subject to a further increase in line with inflation. The boycott of assessment was suspended and it seemed for a while as if there was going to be a lull in the level of my trade union activity.

However, in 2009 I read in the *Morning Star* that the Information Commissioners' Office (ICO), using Schedule 9 of the Data Protection Act, had raided the offices of a secret organisation called 'the Consulting Association' and had seized files on blacklisted building workers. Although they only seized about 5 per cent of the files, these files showed that 44 of the major UK construction companies were involved as members of the conspiracy and that building employers had given information on trade union activists in their employ as well as paying an annual subscription of £3000 and a fee of £2.20 for each inquiry about workers who applied for jobs with them. The ICO had seized files on 3,213 workers. Finally, some concrete proof, I thought, that a formalised blacklist did, indeed, exist in the building industry. However, although I was interested, I didn't take as much interest as I would have done if I had still worked in construction; something that I hadn't done by then for over 25 years. How wrong would I later prove to be.

Back in education, the following year saw a General Election. In the run-up to the General Election the Labour government, with the support of the Conservatives, set up the Browne Review to look at the future funding of Higher Education. It was clear that the Conservatives wanted to substantially increase student fees, whilst Labour were equivocal about such suggestions. At televised hustings, the Liberal Democrat leader, Nick Clegg, said that under no circumstances would he or his party countenance any increase in student fees. Indeed, all 57 Liberal Democrat MPs signed the National Union of Students' (NUS) pledge to 'agree to vote against any increase in tuition fees during the next Parliament and pressure the government to introduce a fairer alternative.' The Conservatives won the General Election, but did not have an overall majority in parliament to enable them to form a government. The Liberal Democrats subsequently entered into a coalition with the Conservatives in order to enable them to govern.

The NUS had been organising protests in universities and colleges throughout Britain for some time in anticipation of increases to student fees. In the event, the new government made cuts to the budgets of all departments, but whilst most of those cuts were in the region of 15 per cent, the cut to Higher Education funding was 80 per cent. Clearly, universities could not sustain their level of provision unless they could raise money from elsewhere. The government proposed increasing the cap on student fees from £3,290 to £9,000 and, although 21 Liberal Democrat MPs rebelled and voted against the increase, it was not enough to stop it going through. It also meant 40 per cent cuts to teaching budgets in order for universities to remain financially viable. The Liberal Democrat leadership had shown their true colours as 'light blues' who couldn't be trusted.

In response, the NUS and UCU organised a march and rally in central London to protest about this. Myself, several of my colleagues and a good number of my students attended the march and rally. The scale of the protest defied expectations, with the most conservative estimates putting the number of protestors turning out to vent their anger at 50,000. The vast majority of protesters were peaceful, and those at the front of the march watched videos and heard impassioned speeches against the cuts. Footage of the deputy prime minister, Nick Clegg, promising to scrap tuition fees was greeted by abusive chants.

Of course, the mainstream media, as they always do, focused on a small minority of protestors (agents provocateurs?) who broke off from the main route of the march, occupied the lobby of the Conservative Party headquarters, smashed windows and waved anarchist flags from the roof of the building. No mention was made by the mainstream media in subsequent reports that this action was totally condemned by the organisers of the rally as well as by the vast majority of protestors. Plus ca change!

Meanwhile, in parliament, Nick Clegg, who deputised for David Cameron at prime minister's questions, came under sustained attack. The deputy Labour leader, Harriet Harman, said she hoped Clegg would go and tell the students protesting outside parliament how 'fair' the government's plan was. Harman said: 'In April, he [Clegg] said that increasing tuition fees to £7,000 a year would be a disaster. What word would he use to describe fees of £9,000?' Clegg claimed that there was a 'consensus' across the parties about the need to reform the system. Despite their own duplicity, Harman on behalf of the Labour Party, replied: 'None of us agree with tuition fees of £9,000 a year.' Tellingly, she didn't say what increase the Labour Party would agree to. Despite the ultimate failure of the protestors to effect change, there was a noticeable change with regard to the 'politicisation' of many of my own students who had attended the march and rally; not that anyone would have thought that sociology students would have needed politicising!

This was perhaps the most pleasing aspect of this march and rally over the many others that I had attended over the course of my working life; and there had been so many, that I've forgotten most of them. In 2013, at the age of 65, I retired from full-time work. Although I fully intended to remain a trade union member, I thought that my activism would be much reduced in future. How wrong could I be!

Chapter 10

Retirement? Activism returns!

No sooner had I retired in 2013 than when my old friend from undergraduate days, Liz, who was now the course leader for sociology at Anglia Ruskin University in Cambridge, asked me if I could teach research methods to post-graduates on their MA Sociology course as an Associate Lecturer. Associate Lecturers work on an hourly paid basis and are normally contracted for a module or modules. I agreed and this started five years of teaching at Anglia Ruskin University on sociology undergraduate and post-graduate programmes as well as on the Public Services degree programme. I became leader for undergraduate modules 'Contemporary Work and Organisations' and 'Making Sense of Popular Culture' as well as leader for masters' modules in 'Cultural Theory and Popular Culture' and 'Post-Graduate Research Methods'. Whilst I transferred my UCU membership to Cambridge branch, I never really became too involved in union activity in the branch, which was well-organised anyway.

Indeed, my trade union activity went in a completely different and totally unexpected direction. Out of the blue, I was flabbergasted to receive a letter from the Information Commissioners' Office (ICO) telling me that when they had raided the offices of the Consulting Association four years earlier in 2009 that one of the 3,213 construction industry blacklist files that they had seized was a file that was being held on me, more than 25 years since I had last worked in the construction industry! The letter asked me if I would like a copy of this file. The file had originally been made by the Economic League which was formed just after World War I to blacklist workers in all industries. After the 1972 National Building Workers' strike, an offshoot, the so-called 'Services Group', had been set up to specifically target active trade unionists in the building industry.

After the Economic League had been forced to shut down by a Parliamentary Inquiry in 1993, the company *Sir Robert McAlpine Ltd*, or more specifically their CEO, Cullum McAlpine, had bought their blacklist database for £10,000 and had invested a further £10,000 in setting up another secret organisation called the Consulting Association. They had installed Ian Kerr, former employee of the Economic League to manage the organisation. Despite many building workers who were active trade unionists claiming that they still couldn't get work, proposed legislation against blacklisting by the 'New Labour' government was shelved both in 1999 and 2003 after assurances were given to MPs by construction companies that the practice had ceased since the closing down of the Economic League. Once again, it was clear that what people in sharp suits and ties said was more 'believable' to the 'New Labour' apparatchiks than what people in donkey jackets said.

I applied for my file and discovered on receiving it that the company that had originally blacklisted me was none other than *MJ Gleeson*, the company whose senior executives had laughed at me and told me that, like other trade union activists, I was paranoid when I mentioned the blacklist. Like many other so-called 'respectable businessmen', *MJ Gleeson* executives were obviously congenital liars. I had learned over many years not to let a sharp suit and tie fool me! On the file, they described me as 'intransigent and militant' (the original was underlined like this); hence the title of this book.

However, as can be seen from the image above, the names of the actual people who had blacklisted me had been redacted on the files. The ICO claimed that this was because to reveal their names might breach their human rights! What about my human rights not to have my personal information misused? Like other affected workers, I joined forces with the Blacklist Support Group (BSG). The BSG had been set up in 2010 by 10 affected workers to work independently of, but also within their trade unions, UCATT, UNITE and the GMB, to fight this long-standing injustice. The campaign quickly grew as other affected workers like me received their files, although the ICO had to be forced to provide workers with the files that they now had on them that they had received. It had taken them four years before they provided me with my file, which I had received eventually only because of the persistence of a handful of dedicated members of the BSG.

FAWBERT John Keith   8.7.48

23 Grange Rd.,   YL 33 91 45 B
Aveley
Essex

Crpenter

1978 May 15th Information from ███████████ Gleesons that they have employed subject
              ontheir Littlebrook Site over the last 2 years and they have found him
              particularly intransigent and militant,The job finishes in a short
              while and they hope to be rid of him then (Source 559)

1980 July 9th. ████████ phoned today to tell us that subject has now left their
                employment. (Source 559) He worked on the Dartford Power Station.

From my blacklist file

Over the next few years, I attended meetings of the BSG, mostly in London and
sometimes in House of Commons Committee Rooms, thanks to the support given by a
handful of Labour MPs. John McDonnell in particular was unstinting in his support,
asking questions in the House, providing Committee Rooms and joining us on
demonstrations and the like, despite the fact that he was a very busy parliamentarian as a
result of being appointed by the new Labour leader, Jeremy Corbyn, to the Shadow
Cabinet as Shadow Chancellor in 2015.

When Jeremy Corbyn was elected to lead Labour, I joined the party, thinking that now
we had a leader who would transform the party from its 'Blairite' incarnation into a
genuine socialist party committed to radical change. Indeed, in his first Labour Party
conference speech as leader, the first thing that he vowed to do was to get justice for
blacklisted workers. During what was to become my five years in the Labour Party, I was
elected by the North-West Suffolk branch as a delegate to the Eastern Regional
Conference, stood unsuccessfully as the party's candidate in the County Council elections
and was elected as the party's liaison representative to the West Suffolk TUC; more about
the latter later. Because of deteriorating health, I didn't join in as many of the activities
of the Labour Party as I would have liked nor in the activities of the BSG; especially, with

regard to the BSG, where picketing on cold and wet days and occupations of construction companies' offices had become rather more taxing ventures for me.

I asked my former union UCATT if they would provide me with legal representation to fight this injustice of being blacklisted. They agreed so long as I re-joined for the period that they would be representing me. They firstly took High Court action to secure the unredacted file, arguing that they couldn't take action against the perpetrators, if they didn't know who they were. Indeed, I don't know of any other crime where the victims are not allowed to know the names of those who committed crimes against them. The judge reluctantly agreed that the unredacted files should be provided to the victims, their trade unions and the lawyers representing them, but that they should not be made public.

In a cynical public relations exercise the criminals set up the pitiful 'Construction Workers' Compensation Scheme' (CWCS) that even they admitted would have resulted in most blacklisted workers receiving just £1000. The conditions attached to accepting the 'compensation', such as dropping all accusations of blacklisting against employers, were totally unacceptable. Like other blacklisted workers, when the ICO had sent me my file it was also accompanied by a letter advising me to contact the employers about the scheme. This was despite the fact that it had been dismissed by both the trade unions and the BSG as a totally inadequate stunt designed to merely distract attention away from their criminality, to keep the case out of court and to placate concerned MPs. In fact, the employers even tried to dupe MPs into falsely believing that this scheme had been agreed with the trade unions. Steve Murphy, General Secretary of UCATT, said that 'the ICO's advice is like telling someone who is in debt to visit a loan shark.' (Morning Star, 12 April, 2014).

Such blatant lies by the employers were condemned by MPs, including even some Conservative MPs such as Simon Revell, who said that the employers' assertions were 'intended to mislead every Member of Parliament' by falsely claiming that unions and the BSG supported it. As a consequence, the employers promised to amend the scheme. In the event, all they did was increase the amount that most claimants would get to £4,000. The employers then sent a letter to all claimants, including me, offering this increased amount. I sent a letter back to them saying the following:

Jeremy Corbyn speaking at the Burston Strike School Rally.

With the West Suffolk delegation to the Labour Party Eastern Region conference in 2020

127

£4000 from you criminals for decades of human-rights abuses that forced many decent people, including myself, out of the industry, leading to me suffering years of deprivation to build another career in education, seeing my kids on free school meals and the family nearly splitting up. And for what? For simply representing my fellow workers on a building site as a UCATT shop steward and legally appointed safety rep. This PR stunt makes no admission of guilt or gives me an apology for what you did to me and my family (cited in Smith & Chamberlain, 2015: 365).

Most blacklisted workers felt the same and very few accepted the offer, deciding instead to continue with litigation. Because of the inadequacies of the tribunal system, multiple claims in the High Court against *Sir Robert McAlpine Ltd* were launched for offences including defamation, breaches of the 1998 Data Protection Act, conspiracy and misuse of private information. Initially, this had been done by legal representatives *Guney, Clarke and Ryan* (GCR) in 2012 on a 'no win, no fee' basis for the first litigants because the unions had not agreed to represent the workers in High Court action. Once this was started, however, they were joined by solicitors acting on behalf of UCATT, UNITE and the GMB.

This is where I came in. In July 2014 the judge hearing the cases agreed that construction companies involved in blacklisting had a case to answer and that 771 separate cases made by victims of blacklisting, including myself, should be heard together under a Group Litigation Order (GLO). The case was to be managed by a Steering Committee comprising solicitors acting for the unions UCATT, UNITE and GMB as well as GCR for the BSG against a consortium of eight of the UK's largest construction companies, known as the 'McFarlane Defendants'.

Case management hearings proceeded to take two years, with the employers' lawyers using every delaying tactic imaginable. I attended almost all of those hearings in the High Court in London, demonstrating along with other BSG members outside the court beforehand, often with the support of the Shadow Chancellor, John McDonnell, and sitting in the public gallery to hear the obstructive and miserable excuses for such despicable behaviour by the employers' representatives. At first, they denied everything. When confronted with the evidence, they then claimed that it was merely a 'vetting scheme' to advise employers on the best workers available. It's funny that I was put on this list of 'undesirables' by the same employer that had told me that I was one of the best carpenters that had ever worked for them! Lawyers representing the employers prevaricated from hearing to hearing when ordered to supply the court with documents.

Eventually, as a full trial date inched ever closer, in 2016 they settled out of court and were forced to give a grovelling, if insufficient, public apology. I, like the others, received compensation. However, compensation is not the same as justice. I was lucky to remain relatively unscathed by the blacklist, finding another career. Many workers went years without work, brought their children up in poverty, experienced family breakdown and divorce and suffered mental illness. And for what? For simply being trade union members and trying to get better wages and conditions for their fellow workers as well as trying to prevent them from being killed on construction sites. In addition, employers are still blacklisting building workers.

So, the struggle went on. In February 2016 I presented a paper entitled 'Blacklisted! A History of Rank-and-File Class Struggle on Construction Sites' to the 'Before 68: the Left, Activism and Social Movements in the Long 1960s' conference at the University of East Anglia. As a consequence of that, I submitted and had published an article with the same title to the peer-reviewed academic journal *Socialist History* Vol. 50 (2016). I appeared in the short film *Apologies*, directed by Lucy Parker (2016) about the so-called 'apology' given by lawyers representing the employers and later was to have a small part in her film *Solidarity* (2019), which had its premiere at the Sheffield International Documentary Festival (the *Sheffield DocFest*) that I went to. I was also a guest on BBC Radio 4's 'Thinking Allowed' programme, having a 15-minute interview with presenter, Lawrie Taylor, on the extent and nature of the construction blacklist (http://www.bbc.co.uk/programmes/b07zzrkw).

I also presented the paper 'Blacklisting: A History of Class Struggle on Construction Sites up to 1993' to the 'Blacklisting, Bullying and Blowing the Whistle' conference at the University of Greenwich in September 1993. In early 2017 I had an article entitled 'Blacklisted! A Case Study in Corporate Crime' in the 'A' Level magazine, *Sociology Review* (Vol. 27 No. 1) and in April of that year I presented the paper 'Blacklisted! Personal Troubles of a Construction Milieu to Public Issues of Work in a Capitalist Society' to the British Sociological Association's Annual Conference at the University of Manchester which had the theme 'Recovering the Social: Personal Troubles and Public Issues'. I also gave presentations on the issue at Anglia Ruskin University and Birkbeck College.

Comrades at a BSG meeting, together with Bill Morris, the first black General Secretary of a major trade union; the Transport and General Workers Union.

With fellow blacklisted workers and John McDonnell MP outside the High Court in the Strand

Indeed, I had become more of a 'keyboard warrior' by this time; even more so after suffering a heart attack at home in late 2017. I was taken to West Suffolk Hospital and then on to the world-famous Papworth Hospital in Cambridgeshire where I had operations to put a stent in an artery and had a pacemaker fitted. Although, as I said, I was no longer fit enough to engage in a lot of trade union activity at the coalface as it were, I decided to use what skills I had to spread the message about the extent and perniciousness of blacklisting as far and wide as I could in the labour movement and beyond as possible. I have given presentations to, amongst others, the Trades Councils of West Suffolk, Cambridge, Ipswich and Barking and Dagenham. I have also given presentations on the issue to several Labour Party branches, including West Suffolk and Bury-St-Edmunds as well as to the West Suffolk People's Assembly and the organisation 'Turning Suffolk Red'.

In these presentations, besides talking about my own research and articles, I always promote the book 'Blacklisted: The Secret War Between Big Business and Union Activists' (2016). It is a brilliant and much more detailed exposition of the shocking and widespread conspiracy against building workers by the capitalist class up until 2016 than I could ever give. It is a must read for any trade union activist. It is written by the secretary of the BSG and fellow West Ham United supporter, Dave Smith, and the journalist, Phil Chamberlain.

As I said earlier, the issue hasn't gone away and there have been many developments not only in the scale and nature of blacklisting over recent years, but also developments exposing the extent of the conspiracy; too many to go into here, but just to say that at the time of writing there are two separate enquiries going on; one into the role of the police and one into the role of corrupt trade union officials in the conspiracy; the latter of which I have contributed to. Every time I am invited to do a new presentation, I update it to include the latest developments. I have also been asked by solicitors to help as an expert witness and have contributed to claims by individuals for past blacklisting offences on a number of occasions; claims that I am delighted to say have resulted in considerable sums of compensation being awarded to litigants.

Back in academia, the 2017-2018 academic year witnessed the start of the most sustained and widespread industrial action by lecturers to have taken place at British universities in their history. UCU launched industrial action over proposed changes to the Universities Superannuation Scheme (USS) at those universities (pre-1992 universities) where the scheme was in operation. Employers were represented by Universities UK (UUK). I was not personally involved in this, but I supported the action by my former colleagues in the so-called 'traditional universities' sector. I was still the external examiner for the Sociology undergraduate programme at the University of Ulster in Derry, Northern Ireland and, in line with UCU policy, I, along with 700 others, resigned in solidarity with my colleagues to try to put pressure on the employers to negotiate. This, combined with strikes and occupations of campus buildings by students in support of striking staff at more than a dozen universities, succeeded in preventing the abolition of defined-benefit pensions in the USS scheme.

At the end of the 2017-2018 academic year, after five years of working as an Associate Lecturer at Anglia Ruskin University, I decided to call it a day. I thought that I didn't really want or need the pressure of the work, albeit on a part-time basis, any longer. Later that same year UCU launched industrial action over pay equality, workloads, casualisation, and pay levels (dubbed the 'Four Fights'), across the whole university sector. The employers were represented by the Universities and Colleges Employers Association (UCEA). In addition, because it was suspended during the Covid crisis, industrial action was set to rumble on for years over these four issues right up to the time of writing this book and eventually, it was set to involve me directly; but more about that later.

During my 'second retirement' I saw that the Workers' Educational Association (WEA) were looking for part-time tutors to teach leisure courses and I thought that this would be much more relaxing and enjoyable. I devised and tutored courses on 'What is criminology?', 'What is society?' and, a passion of mine, 'The social history of Association Football' at a variety of locations around East Anglia before the pandemic and online once Covid restrictions came into force. However, the most exciting development was being offered by the WEA the chance to tutor an 'Organising for Health and Safety' course for UNISON in Ipswich. I was assured that if this went well, I would be offered further courses by UNISON. As I hadn't taught health and safety for quite some time, I had a lot of reading and preparation to do before the course, especially on changes to legislation in the intervening years. However, this was very much a labour of love.

Students on the course were UNISON-appointed Safety Reps. from a very wide spectrum of occupations; amongst others, there were paramedics, coach drivers and local authority grass cutters. I really enjoyed tutoring the course, especially as I was amongst very like-minded people. I was highly praised by the students, as well as by monitors from both UNISON and the WEA, for the innovative and professional way that I went about the more student-centred teaching and learning that is a hallmark of trade union education. Despite this, disappointingly, for a number of reasons, including the onset of COVID restrictions, I didn't get any more UNISON courses to tutor.

It was now 2019 and it wasn't a great year for me. In February of that year, I suffered a second heart attack whilst at a West Ham game at the London Stadium.

With John McDonnell at a Blacklist Support Group meeting in the House of Commons.

With Jeremy Corbyn at the Burston Strike School Rally in 2019

I was taken to Barts Hospital where they had to stop my heart before performing life-saving surgery and I was kept in hospital for a fortnight. Also, after the Labour Party were badly beaten at a General Election, Jeremy Corbyn announced that he was going to stand down as leader. During his time as leader, he had built a mass socialist party of more than half a million members. At the 2017 General Election Labour had increased its share of the vote to 40 per cent, with its 9.6 per cent vote rise being their largest improvement since the 1945 General Election. This so surprised and worried the ruling class that they launched a vicious campaign of hate and lies against the Labour leader and his supporters inside and outside of parliament.

The vitriol of the mainstream media in particular was on a scale rarely seen against the leader of any mainstream political party. Worse still was the complicity in this campaign of lies by Labour Party Central Office. The subsequent *Forde Report* highlighted the extent and viciousness of this treachery. No wonder that the party were routed at the 2019 General Election. I would encourage anyone who has any doubts about the scale and reach of the campaign to vilify Jeremy Corbyn and his supporters by agencies of the state, the mainstream media and Labour Party Head Office to try to get to see the film *Oh, Jeremy*

Corbyn: The Big Lie (Reeves, 2023); not easy as the ruling class have done all it can to get it banned from being shown, even to the extent that it was banned at the *Glastonbury* and *Tolpuddle* festivals.

Also, it is no wonder that the party were encouraged by the establishment to elect a 'safer' leader in Sir Kier Starmer. In 2020, the new leadership chose to ignore the recommendations of the *Forde Report*. Indeed, the party moved sharply to the right. A number of decisions made me question whether or not, as a life-long socialist, I could remain a member of the Labour Party. A series of decisions by the leadership of the party eventually prompted me to pen the following resignation letter to my local party branch, which I reproduce here in full:

It is with a heavy heart that I write this letter to you. I feel that the time has come when I can no longer remain a member of the Labour Party. As I have always said, I've been an active trade unionist and socialist all my adult life. I have 55 years continuous trade union membership, always paid the political levy and always voted Labour. I joined the Labour Party when Jeremy Corbyn was elected because I thought that we now had a genuine socialist leading the Labour Party.

During the last five years I have become increasingly disillusioned. Corbyn was undermined by the party machine from the first day he took office. The suspensions and expulsions of Chris Williamson, Marc Wadsworth and Jackie Walker, all good socialists, on flimsy excuses and trumped-up charges under the leadership of McNichol, were early signs of the ruthlessness and viciousness of the right-wing in the party.

The report on the way that the right-wing undermined Corbyn during his tenure as party leader revealed astonishing levels of bullying, harassment and racism against such fine comrades as Dianne Abbott and anyone deemed to be 'a trot'. Yet nothing has been done to even censure these people, let alone suspend them.

As you know, I was blacklisted by construction employers for 30 years. The Security Services were illegally supplying information on trade union activists like me to the blacklisting employers. Even more seriously, they duped women who were environmental activists into having relationships with them; at least one of them bore a child by an undercover officer, unaware that he worked in the security services and was married with children of his own. That was, effectively, legally sanctioned rape by the state.

So, I was absolutely appalled at Starmer's decision to whip Labour MPs to abstain on the latest Security Bill. This legislation will allow the security services to do the same and break the law with impunity without fear of prosecution. And Starmer is an ex-human rights lawyer! 30 honourable Labour MPs defied the whip and voted against the bill along with all 45 SNP MPs. It is pertinent to point out that the inquiry into the previous abuses of human rights started this week after the state had managed to delay proceedings for six years.

Now we come to the latest violation of natural justice; Jeremy Corbyn's suspension. Corbyn's 'crime' was to say "One anti-Semite is one too many, but the scale of the problem was also dramatically overstated for political reasons by our opponents inside and outside the party, as well as by much of the media." Not only do most Labour Party members agree with that, including myself, but also the EHRC report specifically states that Labour Party members, under the terms of the European Human Rights Convention, can "express their opinions on internal Party matters, such as the scale of antisemitism within the party, based on their own experience and within the law."

In all my years as a trade unionist and a socialist I have never once heard a Labour Party member make an anti-Semitic remark or take any action that could be construed as anti-Semitic. I have been both a lay and full-time trade union official and I have mixed with Labour Party members at work, at conferences and socially all my life. Since becoming a member of the Labour Party five years ago I have never encountered any anti-Semitism at branch, CLP or Trades Council meetings. There is absolutely no doubt in my mind that the problem has been grossly over-exaggerated. Am I not allowed to say so? I remain committed to fighting anti-Semitism, but, spurred on by the apologists for the apartheid regime in Israel, who are opposed to his support for the Palestinians, anti-Semitism has been used as a stick to beat Jeremy Corbyn with by the right-wing of the party.

Corbyn has done more to combat all forms of racism during his lifetime than all his opponents in the Labour Party put together. He has been arrested on picket lines for opposing racism and to those who say that his anti-racism stance has not included opposing anti-Semitism, they need to look at Hansard. Since becoming an M.P. he has put down or supported Early Day Motions condemning anti-Semitism on more than 40 occasions.

The right for party members to express an opinion is what is clearly being challenged by Keir Starmer, who has said that those who "pretend" that anti-Semitism is "exaggerated or factional are part of the problem". The context of Corbyn's comments were a reference to an opinion poll which suggested that the public believed as many as a third of Labour's 600,000 members were "anti-Semitic"; something that is clearly an exaggeration. In the aftermath of Corbyn's suspension, we had a Labour MP tweeting about a "tidal wave" of anti-Semitism in the Party. So, it seems to be acceptable for the media and right-wing Labour MPs, to grossly overstate the scale of the problem, but not acceptable for Party members to say the opposite.

Although the suspension is said to have come from the Labour general secretary, David Evans, few Party members believe it could have happened without consultation with Keir Starmer. Indeed, Starmer has explicitly stated that he supports the decision. Few will believe that suspending Corbyn for doing something the EHRC report explicitly says he has a right to do, is anything other than a blatant political manoeuvre. Indeed, Labour members will be forgiven for thinking that Starmer had been waiting for an excuse, however small or contrived, to get rid of Corbyn.

The right-wing say that he was given the chance to apologise and retract his statement and that he still has the chance to do so. So, they are expecting him to be dishonest like Galileo denouncing the heliocentric view of the solar system in front of the inquisition, are they? What sort of party is this? There are those that say 'stay and fight, otherwise the right-wing have won'. Until recently, I was one of those people, but with this latest development I can no longer justify to myself staying in a political party that continues with its witch-hunt against socialists.

All my adult life I have been told that the Labour Party is a 'broad church'. Yet, the witch-hunt against the left in the Party has now reached levels comparable to the tactics of McCarthy. Starmer calls this 'uniting the party', but the party can never be united when a purge of the left continues unabated. When leader, Jeremy Corbyn, for all his faults, tried really hard to unite the party by bringing people like Hilary Benn and Kier Starmer into his Shadow Cabinet, his reward was to be stabbed in the back by these people (Benn with his support for US bombing of Syria and Starmer by undermining Labour's policy on Brexit).

Perhaps if Jeremy Corbyn has faults it is that he is too kind, compassionate and gentle for his own good. But, then, that is, for me, what good socialists should be like. Unfortunately, the Labour Party is now further away from representing those values than ever.

In resigning from the party, I want to make it absolutely clear that I have no ill-feelings towards any members of the North-West Suffolk branch or the West Suffolk CLP. Over the last five years I have met some wonderful comrades who I now also count as good friends. I hope that we can remain so. We do have our differences, but I'd like to think that we have always expressed them in a comradely way. I have, indeed, been proud to represent the branch and CLP as a County Council candidate, at the West Suffolk Trades Council and at the Eastern Region Labour Party conference.

Sadly, I got no response to my letter of resignation. I also sent a copy to Head Office and all I got back was a standard letter regretting my decision to leave the party. There was no attempt to address the reasons for my decision. Like many comrades who left the party, I decided to concentrate on trade union activity. As I was a member of West Suffolk Trades Council by virtue of being the Liaison Officer from the local Labour Party, I thought that I would now have to resign from that position. However, the other members of the Trades Council persuaded me to continue as a member representing my trade union, UCU, instead; something that I have been proud to do to this day.

Chapter 11

From activist to supporter?

B y now, I was much more of a supporter of trade unionism than an activist. In 2021, I noticed that the Open University were advertising for Associate Lecturers on an hourly paid basis to tutor students online for a number of modules. As I had taught criminology as a Senior Lecturer, especially at De Montfort University and the University of Bedfordshire, I applied to tutor on two of the criminology modules. At interview, I accepted that it might be a good idea if I started with just one module and so I was accepted to tutor a group of students on line on a second-year module entitled 'Understanding Criminology'. I decided to give up the teaching for the WEA, especially as the organisation were returning to face-to-face teaching after the pandemic. However, I did continue to give one or two 'members' lectures' when asked to.

As the pandemic was 'over' and much of university teaching was returning to face-to-face tuition, UCU also resumed industrial action, together with UNISON and UNITE at a number of institutions. Widely observed strike days were 1st to the 3rd December 2021, 14th February to 2nd March 2022 and 21st March to 1st April. As I was only 'tutoring' part-time for one module just a few hours a week and, as the times I decided to do this were flexible, I had to make the difficult decision to declare to the Open University which of the strike days I would 'normally' have been working. Because, for me, there was no such thing as 'normal working' on any day (I worked on, for example, marking students' work when I felt like it), I decided to declare that I was on strike on a pro-rata basis, thus having the same percentage deduction from my pay as all my full-time colleagues. These strikes led to a variety of local agreements between individual universities and union branches.

One of the issues about which we were taking action was the issue of the casualisation of the Higher Education workforce. Universities were using hourly-paid Associate Lecturers more and more to deliver courses and this had been happening over a number of years. It had now got to the point where some universities were using more 'casual' staff in this way than securely employed staff. The University sector had become part of the 'gig economy'. Nevertheless, agreement was reached between the Open University and the OU UCU branch to employ all Associate Lecturers on part-time permanent contracts.

However, casualisation was only one part of the dispute with the employers. The dispute was also about pay, workloads and equality pay gaps. In addition, there was a second dispute over cuts to the pension scheme. It was a dispute that I enthusiastically supported. So, action resumed in the 2022/23 academic year. For the first time in the dispute, UCU secured a mandate for industrial action at all

In 2022 I was continuing to campaign against the blacklisting of building workers. This is a presentation that I gave to Suffolk People's Assembly.

UCU rally in London in 2022 that I attended.

UK branches. Thus, I took part in the strikes that were organised for the 24th to 25th of November and the 30th November 2022.

Into 2023, there were also 12 days of strike action in February and March that I took part in. Other days when strike action was planned were cancelled in order to enable negotiations to take place with the body representing the employers. On 15th March 2023, it was announced that negotiations with 'Universities UK', the body responsible for negotiating over pensions, promised the restoration of pension terms comparable with 2017 levels, whilst the 'Universities and Colleges Employers Association' (UCEA), the body responsible for negotiating with UCU over the so-called 'Four Fights' dispute, offered to 'agree new standards, frameworks and principles to tackle other forms of casualised contracts, reduce workloads and close equality pay gaps.' On 17th April 2023, UCU, satisfied with progress made in the talks, paused industrial action concerning pensions, but a marking and assessment boycott (MAB) was declared with regard to the 'Four Fights' dispute.

At my own university, the Open University, as at many others, the response to the MAB was patchy and half-hearted. Because of Tory legislation outlawing the closed shop, not every lecturer was a trade union member and some of those who were members were refusing to take part in the MAB. Despite being forced to conduct ballots on industrial action that have very strict rules because of Tory legislation and getting an overwhelming vote in favour of such action, one had to ask why these scabs were still allowed to continue with membership of the union?

Furthermore, staff who hadn't fulfilled all their hours were being told to make them up with marking the work of those who were participating in the MAB. Many of these substitute markers were not au fait with the modules they were marking, and sometimes not even with the subject that they were assessing, so the quality of marking was severely diminished. In addition, this was driving a wedge between fellow workers who had to work together when the dispute was over. Some comrades were suggesting that the MAB should be abandoned in favour of all-out strike action.

Consequently, UCUs Higher Education Committee consulted members and 60 per cent of those voting indicated that they were in favour of suspending the MAB. Other actions short of strike action were to continue. These included working to contract, not covering for absent colleagues, removing uploaded materials related to, and/or not sharing materials related to, lectures or classes that were cancelled as a result of strike action, not rescheduling lectures or classes cancelled due to strike action, and not undertaking any voluntary activities. The Higher Education Committee also called five days of strike action from Monday 25th to Friday 29th September 2023. Some branches arranged for local variations to ensure that they could coordinate with other campus unions or to manage their own local disputes on punitive pay deductions or redundancies.

It was announced that branches could, if they wished, withdraw from the national strike action. On the basis that the OU branch decided that it would only stand down as a result of concessions over the MAB and disputes, the Executive Committee of the branch announced that they would attempt to have talks with the university about a deal. One starting point was asking that MAB deductions be returned as had happened at Sussex University (or capped, as elsewhere) but they were also exploring if there was any way that they could make progress on local aspects of the Four Fights. No progress was made so, following a vigorous debate at a very full branch meeting on 20th September, the branch voted not to stand down strike action from Monday 25th until Friday 29th September. The one-week strike went ahead in what was effectively 'freshers' week'.

On 5th October, however, justice prevailed in UCU's long fight for USS pensions. The employers' representative body Universities UK (UUK) agreed to reverse the 35% cut made to the Universities Superannuation Scheme (USS) and to restore what had been lost. This was worth between £15bn and £17bn, as well as an additional one-off pension payment of around £900m to make up for the benefits that USS members had lost. The agreement also paved the way for new contribution rates to be introduced. The USS trustees showed that it was sustainable to restore benefits and to keep the new contribution rates for at least two pension valuation cycles (six years). The agreement was recommended unanimously by UCU's negotiators and the UCU's elected members on the Higher Education Committee. A full members vote ratified the decision. Victory! As the OU UCU branch said in an email to all members: 'It's one of the biggest pension wins for any union, ever.'

It is worth noting that in 2018, when the employers had attempted to close the defined benefit part of USS pensions and to move everyone to defined contribution, the chorus of employers, politicians and mainstream media commentators had told us that this was inevitable. UCU members, however, wouldn't accept the voices of the establishment and had fought back in huge numbers to protect their pensions. In 2022, the employers had forced through completely unnecessary cuts to USS pensions, using a flawed pension valuation conducted at the height of the Covid-19 pandemic.

The same chorus of employers, politicians and mainstream media commentators told us that this had to happen, and that winning back our pensions would be an impossible task. Again, we had refused to give in and it was reversed because the whole union pulled together and refused to accept these lies. After 69 days of strike action, years of campaigning, protesting and lobbying, we achieved an historic victory. It showed, once again, that workers should never believe what those in the establishment in sharp suits tell them. It also showed what solidarity could achieve and it should be motivation for every single worker in the United Kingdom who has seen their pension slashed to fight back.

However, the Tory government attacks on trade unions and on education in particular continued. On 28 October 2023, Michelle Donelan MP, the Secretary of State for Science, Innovation and Technology wrote to UK Research and Innovation (UKRI) criticising two UCU members who were also members of the UKRI's Equality, Diversity and Inclusion board (EDI) for social media comments that they had made over events in Israel and Palestine. Donelan's comments were an outrageous misrepresentation of the academics' posts and a deliberately provocative direct intervention to try to curtail the freedom of expression that British academics were traditionally entitled to.

Instead of resisting such government interference in academic freedom of expression, UKRI decided to suspend the EDI advisory board. This was a clear attack on academic freedom of expression and the professionalism of academic staff that goes against everything that academia has stood for over centuries. On 30th October, the UCU General Secretary, Jo Grady wrote to UKRI giving them until 3rd November to give an assurance that they would reverse this decision, or all UCU members would withdraw from all advisory positions within UKRI. No such assurance was received.

Also, the 'four fights' dispute was set to continue with a ballot for further industrial action. However, despite UCU members voting overwhelmingly in favour of both strike action and action short of a strike, the wishes of the membership fell foul of the Tory imposed anti-union laws. In the ballot, more than two-thirds of those voting, voted for strike action and over three-quarters voted for action short of a strike. Yet, because the turnout was less than 50%, it would be illegal under the Tory legislation to go ahead with industrial action. This anti-trade union legislation makes the wholly unwarranted assumption that those who didn't vote were against industrial action. Why isn't the same criterion applied to parliamentary elections to those who make these anti-union laws and, as the General Secretary of UCU, Jo Grady, said in an email to all members informing them of the result:

It is sickening that tens of thousands of workers can vote for strike action and have this deemed illegal by a government led by somebody that nobody voted for [Rishi Sunak].

Nevertheless, the employers' body, UCEA, recognising the strength of feeling of UCU members, indicated that they were prepared to enter into extensive negotiations with the union on a range of issues, including pay. However, the employers have said this in the past, as I recounted earlier, and it's proved to be a false dawn. Employers never change their spots! In addition, UCU also discovered that government employees were compiling secret dossiers on UCU members. I thought, here we go again! Blacklisting all over again.

The fight for justice on pay, working conditions and job security for UCU members continued. Due to the health issues that I mentioned earlier, I have not been as involved in these recent struggles as much as I would like to have been. These days, as I said, I am more of a supporter than an activist, but we all do what we can and I will continue to support my union until the day I finally depart this world, despite the fact that I may disagree from time to time with decisions made by the leadership of my union; that is what solidarity means. It doesn't mean unconditional support as long as there are democratic processes in place in which to express dissent.

At the time of writing, the UCU struggle over pay and conditions was just one dispute among many in several different sectors of the economy. From 2021 onwards there was an upsurge in trade union militancy on a scale not seen since the 1970s. Postal workers, railway workers, teachers and various NHS workers, amongst many others, were forced to act to protect their members from the 'cost of greed' crisis perpetuated by the capitalist class that saw inflation soar. As a Trades Council member, I played at least a small part as much as I was able to in supporting workers in other sectors by organising meetings and standing in solidarity with them on picket lines when the weather and my health permitted. During this period, I became President of the Trades Council.

Rather than confront the real causes of the crisis, the greed of the capitalist class, the Tory government, not unexpectedly, attacked workers for trying to protect their own interests. Over at least the last 50 of my 60 years of involvement in trade unions, governments led by Tories from Heath to Sunak have introduced increasingly draconian measures to try to curtail the democratic right of workers to combine to protect and advance their wages and conditions. Unfortunately, Labour governments, whilst always opposing Tory legislation, have not repealed most of these restrictions when in office. The trade unions, for their part, have largely acquiesced, albeit reluctantly, to these restrictions on their democratic rights. The Labour Party, under its present leader, Keir Starmer, are likely to continue this trend, if and when they get elected.

At the time of writing the Tory government were pushing through legislation to force workers to work during strikes or face dismissal. Employers will be given the right to name individuals who would be expected to cross picket lines in order to enforce 'minimum service level requirements' across the NHS, schools, public transport and other key sectors. Picket supervisors will be charged with the responsibility to inform all the other pickets not to prevent these workers from going into work. Any worker who refused to cross a picket line could be stripped of their employment rights and sacked by an employer. In other words, strikes for some workers were to be made illegal. It was clear that the whole purpose of this legislation was to render effective strike action unlawful, something that was criticised by the UN agency, the International Labour Organisation (ILO). The ILO's Committee on Freedom of Association had stated that while minimum service levels can be imposed in certain cases, the extent of the minimum services should not render the strike ineffective or call it into question.

A CWU picket line I attended in Bury-St- Edmunds during their 2023 dispute.

An RCN picket line I attended outside West Suffolk Hospital

Surely, this was the time when trade unionists should stand up and challenge this attack on a basic human right, not just in the courts but also in the workplaces and on the streets. Labour Deputy Leader, Angela Rayner, speaking in the debate in the House of Commons, called it the 'sacking nurses bill' and described it as an 'outright attack on the fundamental freedoms of British working people.' She promised that Labour would repeal the legislation when they came to power. However, it remained to be seen whether this legislation would go through in the first place and if it did if Labour would, indeed, scrap it when they came to power.

It was time to say 'enough is enough' and to oppose the bi-partisan approach to trade union legislation that has dominated parliamentary politics for most of my 60 years as a trade unionist.

At the TUC conference in 2023 it was resolved not to comply with the legislation if and when it went through. Finally, I thought, we had trade union leaders and TUC delegates who were prepared to take the bull by the horns. If they had done this 40 years earlier under Thatcher's reign we may have stopped the attacks on trade unions in their tracks as the labour movement did in Ted Heath's day. A TUC special Congress on resisting minimum service level legislation took place in December 2023 to 'explore options for non-compliance and resistance' against minimum service legislation.

Importantly the government left the issue of work notices to the discretion of employers, and it would only apply in the first instance to Department for Transport mandated train operators, ambulance workers and other groups of workers, like Border Force staff deemed to be 'key workers'. Consequently, trade unions agreed to write to all employers that they deal with, including devolved administrations in Scotland and Wales and regional mayors to call on them to pledge to never to issue a work notice if there was a dispute. At the time of writing, such guarantees had already come from the Scottish and Welsh governments. If such guarantees were not forthcoming from other organisations, a number of trade union leaders said that they would consider going into dispute with them over that issue.

Indeed, the Rail, Maritime and Transport union (RMT) were very clear that they would not willingly comply with the legislation in whatever ways are practical and would support other unions who engaged in acts of tactical non-compliance. Furthermore, they and other unions called upon the TUC to mobilise mass resistance in a national demonstration in early 2024 with a view to bringing out workers from every community and walk of life. At the time of writing, I was preparing myself to support such action. It was clear that the Tory government were reacting to the many successes that trade unions had by sustained industrial action over the 'cost of greed' crisis.

Congress voted unanimously that all trade unions would refuse to tell their members to cross picket lines in defiance of the legislation. Personally, I have never crossed a picket line without the pickets' permission in my life, the same as all self-respecting trade unionists. So, to expect trade unionists to INSTRUCT others to cross their picket lines is fanciful in the extreme! A TUC General Council statement of 15 action points that was agreed by every delegate pledged to back any worker refusing a work notice, to engage in legal challenges to the legislation and to demand that employers that they deal with commit to not issuing work notices.

The legislation provided for fines for trade unions not complying with the law of up to £1 million and sequestration of assets. Where any union faced huge fines or sequestration of assets for non-compliance, the TUC executive agreed to convene to look at 'practical, industrial, financial and/or political backing for that union. TUC General Secretary, Paul Nowak, warned employers, 'You send a work notice to a union, you threaten the right to strike, and you should expect to find 48 unions ready to respond' and a call to an emergency demonstration.

The Special Congress also agreed to mobilise a national march in Cheltenham on January 27th 2024 to commemorate the sacked GCHQ workers who defied a ban on joining a trade union in 1984 and to signal 'defiant opposition to Conservative minimum service levels, trade union restrictions and any threat to the right to strike.' Whilst many delegates rightly waned that the trade unions should not rely on a future Labour government to repeal the law, especially at a time that its leader was praising Margaret Thatcher, it was agreed that the Labour Party would be held to its commitment to repeal the legislation within 100 days of winning a General Election. By the time this book is published, we will hopefully have defeated this pernicious attack on our movement.

Chapter 12

'What has the union ever done for me?'

This brings me to the question that I am frequently asked by those who are not in trade unions and may be hostile to them. 'What has the union ever done for me?' is the question that I have heard more times than I care to remember whenever I've mentioned my long-term commitment to the labour movement. My response has usually been 'You're asking the wrong question there, mate. You should be asking 'What have I ever done for the union?' This is fundamental because those who pose the question 'What has the union ever done for me?' totally misunderstand what trade unions are. They are not external bodies that do things for us. They are, or at least they should be, 'what it says on the tin'; unions or collectives of workers supporting one another.

The misguided view that unions 'do things for us' is not surprising given the way that the mainstream national media portray trade unions. One example is the way that the mainstream national media, saturated as they are with privately educated upper-middle-class journalists, talk to and talk about those elected to serve their members. Jeremy Vine, for example, in all his many media guises, frequently talks about 'union bosses' as if they are somehow 'in charge' of their respective memberships. They are not 'bosses' Jeremy! Some right-wing trade union leaders might like to think that they are, but as Mick Lynch has pointed out on numerous occasions to media hacks who accuse him of disrupting the railways and telling his members to go on strike, the members tell him what they want. The linguist and political activist Noam Chomsky could have a field day with the mainstream media purveyors of bourgeois discourse.

However, sometimes when I am feeling rather more accommodating to the question 'What has the union ever done for me?' I reflect more deeply on changes that trade unions have had on the world of work and society more generally during the 60 years that I have been a trade unionist. If my listener is patient enough, I will answer his/her question in detail, rhetorical though the question often is. Firstly, there is what is called the 'union premium' that is almost universally recognised by labour economists; that workers in highly unionised workplaces, on average, earn more than those working in the same or similar occupations in workplaces that are not unionised. This accords with my own experiences in factories, on building sites and in professional occupations that I have had.

I also reflect on the many changes in employment law that have been won by trade union action; changes that have benefitted every working person, including those who are hostile to trade unions and who don't work in highly unionised workplaces. I hadn't been working long when, against considerable opposition from employers, the trade union movement fought for and won the Redundancy Payments Act (1965) which required employers to consult trade unions when considering redundancies, gave a right to all employees, whether trade unionists or not, to receive notice of redundancy and gave the right to all employees, once again whether members of trade unions or not, to receive compensation for being made redundant. This was a great benefit to building workers in particular, many of whom are itinerant.

When I think back to when I started work in 1964, I worked mainly in factories in the most awful and dangerous conditions where wood machinists expected to lose a finger or two during their working lives and where workers were just 'unlucky' if they lost their lives. On building sites in the 70s, I witnessed deaths and injuries caused by a lack of care by greedy contractors who were only interested in their profits and not in the health and safety of the workers who made those profits for them. Trade unions fought for and got the Health and Safety at Work Act (1974) to at least curtail the worst excesses of this carnage.

However, the biggest impact on health and safety in the workplace came from the enactment of the Safety Reps and Safety Committees Regulations (1978) which gave trade unions the right to appoint workplace safety reps who had the right to time off work on full pay for health and safety training, to inspect their workplaces, to report health and safety issues to their employers and to sit on safety committees. There is no doubt in my mind that, despite the intimidation that many of them have received from employers, the work of thousands of safety reps across the country in all industries, but especially on building sites, over the intervening years has saved the lives of thousands of workers and massively reduced the hundreds of thousands of serious injuries at work. They have raised the standards at all workplaces, whether they are organised workplaces or not. All workers, whether trade union members or not, have thus benefitted from the sterling work that these rank-and-file trade unionists have done.

Today, if I worked on a building site, it is much less likely that I would have to ask 400 workers to go on strike to oppose the sacking of a scaffolder shop steward for refusing to work in an isolated location on his own or to ask them to support the widows of four tunnel miners who lost their lives because of the greed of a company who were already making a fortune from a contract on a construction site. As a result of the work done by trade union appointed safety reps since the 1970s, the death toll on building sites has fallen from roughly 350 a year to roughly 50 a year and death, injury and disease due to workplace activity have all fallen dramatically in all workplaces.

I am also proud to have played a part, albeit a small one, in eliminating asbestos from building sites. I have known a number of building workers who contracted and died from asbestosis, and I have a close friend who I worked with on a number of sites who was recently diagnosed with this deadly disease. Despite our campaigns managing to get the substance banned, it can take decades after using it for it to result in this chronic lung condition. *Cape Asbestos*, the company that produced asbestos sheeting in Barking near my hometown of Dagenham and known to victims of their deadly materials as 'the industrial killing machine', lied for years about the effects of their products. Yet, despite giving £40 million for compensation claims, nobody from the company responsible for murder on an industrial scale has ever gone to prison for their crimes. Compare that to Des Warren getting three years in prison for picketing offences that were trumped up anyway. So, when someone says: 'What has the union ever done for me?' I could quite legitimately reply 'probably saved your life mate!'

Also, the appalling levels of discrimination that I witnessed in my early working life have been challenged and changed through trade union action. Whilst the East London dockers coming out on strike in support of Enoch Powell's infamous speech calling for the repatriation of workers from the Caribbean was a blight on the honourable history of trade union struggle against discrimination, it was far from typical. The Race Relations Act

(1968) was not only partly a result of trade union action, but also it became the precursor of rafts of subsequent legislation protecting BAME workers from discriminatory practices. Again, all workers have benefitted from these measures and, despite many continuing issues, black and Asian workers have generally been able to move on from those dark days that I witnessed both in the workplaces that I worked in as well as at the *Grunwick Film Processing Laboratories* in North London in 1977.

Coming from Dagenham, I also remember only too well the strike at the *Ford Motor Company* by those 850 very brave women sewing machinists for equal pay that was immortalised in the film *Made in Dagenham* (2010). Despite the disgusting levels of ridicule and harassment that they got, they stuck out and won a historic victory that paved the way for the Equal Pay Act (1970). Employers were given five years to gradually implement it, but such was their opposition to it, that most employers did nothing to address the issue until they were forced to in 1975 when the act came into force.

Some might legitimately argue that the fight for equal pay by trade unionists had a much longer history than that, beginning with the matchgirls strike by 200 grossly exploited women at the *Bryant and May* factory in East London in 1888. In the year following that historic strike, the TUC had voted unanimously to fight for equal pay for women and had been doing so ever since; sometimes half-heartedly it must be admitted and sometimes with little support from rank-and-file workers. Nevertheless, despite the seeming victory in 1970 in the long campaign for equal pay, employers did everything that they could to get round the legislation. Many employers designated some jobs, the ones done predominantly by men, as 'more skilled' than the jobs done predominantly by women and so they could continue to pay women less.

So, trade unions fought for and achieved two further pieces of legislation to stop these iniquitous practices; the Sex Discrimination Act (1975) became operative on the same day that the Equal Pay Act did. It prevented employers from offering jobs exclusively to men or women and later on, in an amendment to the Equal Pay Act, that workers should be paid the same regardless of their sex if they were doing 'work of equal value' as established by job evaluation schemes. It was this raft of legislation that enabled me to negotiate the first equal opportunities agreement with a national construction company, *Bovis*, to give young women the chance of taking apprenticeships in the building trades. Whilst there have been many advances in this field, it is still an ongoing battle for equality at work between men and women, as the current dispute that I am involved in as a UCU member with the Universities is testament to.

Paid maternity leave and maternity rights have also been won by trade unions for working women. The UK introduced its first maternity leave legislation through the Employment Protection Act 1975, which was extended through further legislation, such as The Employment Act 1980. However, for the first 15 years, only about half of working women were eligible for it because of long qualifying periods of employment. In 2003, male employees received paid statutory paternity leave for the first time; an entitlement that was extended in January 2010.

Whilst the Additional Paternity Leave Regulations giving male workers the right to paid paternity leave and shared parental paid leave, weren't enacted until 2010 trade unionists had been fighting for both maternity and paternity leave on full pay for more than a century. As I said earlier, as a progressive local government under Labour, the Greater London Council (GLC) had maternity leave provisions in place in the 1970s, but not paternity leave and, as I also said earlier, when I was a shop steward on the GLC site in Harold Hill between 1974 and 1976, the works committee petitioned the council through Ken Livingstone, elected as a Labour councillor in 1973, for paternity leave.

We put it to Ken that, as he declared himself to be a 'feminist', he should be supporting us in this campaign; something that he agreed with. As building workers, there were many young men on site who we thought should get paid paternity leave. Ken was instrumental in getting an agreement from the council that male council employees who became fathers would get two weeks' paid leave; not a lot, but a start. Trade unionists in other workplaces fought for and got similar agreements over the years. As in this case, legislation giving all workers benefits and rights often follow as a result of being established as the norm in trade union organised workplaces.

However, it didn't stop there. The struggle by trade unions to ensure that all workers are treated fairly at work and that the most marginalised groups are protected, continued. It eventually resulted in the Equality Act (2010) which protects workers and puts an onus on employers to make 'reasonable adjustments' to avoid discriminating against groups on the basis of age, disability, gender reassignment, race, religion or belief, sex, sexual orientation, pregnancy or maternity, marriage and civil partnership. Unlike when I first started work in 1964, it now means that workforces in many occupations are more likely to reflect the make-up of communities in general. For personal reasons, I was also pleased to see that neurodiversity was included in the category of 'disabled'.

It also means that many employers, like my own, the Open University, require staff to carry out equality training every two years. However, this is ironic given that the Open University, like all universities are resisting the industrial action being taken as I write this by UCU members over four issues, one of which is, as I said a moment ago, the inequalities that still exist amongst staff in British Universities. So, there is still much more that needs to be done. Indeed, despite the legislation, in many workplaces men still dominate senior roles, women are more likely to work in lower paid occupations, occupational segregation more generally still exists, and the gender pay gap, albeit not so large, is still a reality.

On another issue, today most workers take their annual holidays and Bank Holidays for granted. In the 19th century, the majority of working people had Sundays off, but apart from that the only other time that they got off was during the religious holidays of Christmas and Good Friday. From that time, generation after generation of trade unionists have campaigned for every worker to have paid leave as a right. In the late 19th century trade unions fought for and secured the 'half-day holiday' on Saturdays for most workers and over time a five-day, 40-hour week.

The TUC first began to campaign for annual paid holidays for workers as long ago as 1911. Unions encouraged local organisers to demand more paid holiday from employers and workplace-by-workplace some working people began to get more paid time off. Yet, the law still lagged behind. In 1938, after pressure from the unions and the International Labour Organisation (ILO) that had gone on for years, the government finally passed the Holidays with Pay Act. This Act gave some workers the right to one week of paid holiday per year. This was progress, but it fell short of the two weeks demanded by trade unions; and it did not cover all workers. So, the campaign continued for decades. Slowly, over time, unions won the right to two weeks paid leave for most workers through collective bargaining agreements with individual companies. This is what had been won by the time I started work in 1964.

Still, there were many workers in unorganised or weakly organised workplaces who received little or no paid holiday entitlement. In 1993 the EU gave the right to four weeks' paid holiday to all workers, but John Major's Tory government refused to implement it. Finally, after more than a century of campaigning by unions, the law was changed. On 1 October 1998, the new Labour government, under pressure from the trade unions, implemented the EU working time directive. At a stroke, six million workers got more paid holiday than before and two million of them got their first paid holidays ever. The battle started by trade unionists in the early twentieth century had finally been won; even for those workers who say that they 'don't believe in unions'!

Similarly, it was pressure from trade unions that has seen the number of Bank Holidays increase during my working life. For example, I, like millions of other trade unionists in Britain, always used to take an unpaid holiday on May 1st to celebrate international workers' day, or May Day as it is more popularly known. On many occasions I have celebrated the occasion by attending marches and rallies in the capital. May 1st was originally adopted in 1889 by the International Social Congress to honour workers. The pressure to recognise the contribution that workers make to society finally bore fruit in 1978 when Michael Foot, as Secretary of State for Employment, made it a public holiday, which again is enjoyed by all workers, whether trade unionists or not. However, many workers today are unaware that this history underlies why they get a Bank Holiday at the beginning of May every year because bourgeois forces have tried to distance it from its roots by making the holiday the first Monday in May regardless of whether that is May 1st or not.

Today, many of those who say, 'what has the union ever done for me?' and/or 'I don't believe in unions' are in receipt of a national minimum wage that, whilst not being high enough, is certainly higher than they would be getting if trade unions hadn't fought for over a hundred years for such a minimum standard. Trade unions had won national minimum wages in specific industries through firstly the Trade Boards Act in 1909 and then the Wages Councils Act (1945) that established minimum wages on a sectoral basis. These were dismantled by the Tories, with the final 26 Wages Councils being abolished by the Trade Union Reform and Employment Rights Act (1993). The Wages Councils had protected the incomes of more than two and a half million low-paid workers. Most of these workers were low paid precisely because they worked in workplaces that were weakly organised or not organised at all.

Some trade unionists opposed the introduction of a National Minimum Wage because they felt that this would become a maximum for many employers and workers would not see the need to fight through a trade union for better pay. It was, however, the recognition that those most vulnerable to low pay, especially in many of the expanding service industries, were rarely unionised and were not likely to become so in the near future. Labour came to power in 1997 and, under pressure from the trade unions, implemented the National Minimum Wage Act (1998). The implementation of the Act was, needless to say, opposed by the Conservative Party who argued that it would force many companies to go broke. It's my guess that a majority of those who benefit from there being a National Minimum Wage and who may be hostile to trade unions, are unaware of the role that trade unions played in securing them such a minimum standard of living.

This is not to mention the far better sickness and pension entitlements that trade unions have fought for and won for working people since I started work in1964 that I could go into in detail. Then again, my protagonists who say, 'what has the union ever done for me?' have probably stopped listening to me by now and such details would be lost on them. If they hadn't stopped listening, they sometimes say things like 'Oh well, unions were important in the past, but they are not needed any more'. I've been hearing this faux argument for the last 60 years since I first started work and look at what has been achieved during my working life! In any case, since at least 2010, if not longer, trade unionists have been fighting a rearguard action to retain what they had gained in previous years. They are needed more than ever now. So, if you're reading this and you are not a member of a trade union, it is time you joined up!

Well, that's my story up to 2024. It isn't the end, because in a capitalist society trade unions and trade unionists have to continually fight to defend and advance the wages and conditions of working people. Trade unions are not and can never be revolutionary organisations, so until we have a different kind of society, a broadly 'socialist' one (and we can argue about how we might go about achieving that and what a 'socialist society' might look like), trade union struggle to better the lot of working people will always be necessary.

This year I have decided to stop working altogether and take what I think is a well-earned rest. However, although age and some ill-health has now curtailed much of my trade union activity, I am not about to give up the struggle completely just yet. I hope that I can share the struggle with a new generation of activists and hopefully learn from them about new ways of fighting for better wages and conditions for working people. Before retiring from the Open University though, just before Christmas 2023, I agreed to deliver a presentation entitled 'Blacklisted! Corporate Crime and State Conspiracies' to the university's Social Policy and Criminology Department's seminar series on 8th May, 2024.

Well finally, as this book hopefully illustrates, like many of those good comrades that I have met along my trade union journey, I have made many mistakes; but they have been honest mistakes that I hope that I have learnt from. My wish is that this book will encourage others to come forward and share their stories and light the way for future generations of trade unionists. I look forward to reading those stories.

References

Cameron Report (1967) *Report of a Court of Inquiry into Trade Disputes on the Barbican and Horseferry Road Construction Sites in London*, Cmnd. 3396, HMSO: London.

Clarke L. & Wall C. (2015) 'Omitted from History: Women in the Building Trades', *Researchgate*. Available at: www.researchgate.net/publications/265618344

Cole N. (2010) *Made in Dagenham* [Film], Los Angeles: Paramount Pictures.

Dash J. (1969) *Good Morning, Brothers!* London: Lawrence & Wishart.

Fawbert J. (2016) 'Blacklisted! A History of Rank-and-File Class Struggles on Construction Sites', *Socialist History* Vol. 50.

Fawbert J. (2017) 'Blacklisted! A Case Study in Corporate Crime.' *Sociology Review* Vol.27 No.1.

Fawbert J. (2022) *Growing Up in Dagenham: Recollections of a Baby-Boomer* Independent.

Fowler, A. (2021) 'Publish and Be Damned? Mainstream Media and the Challenge of Whistleblowing Sites', in Ward, S. (ed.) *Handbook of Global Media Ethics* New York: Springer. pp. 877–897.

Gall G. (2017) *Bob Crow: Socialist, Leader, Fighter (A Political Biography)* Manchester: Manchester University Press.

Gall G. (2024) *Mick Lynch: The Making of a Working-Class Hero* Manchester: Manchester University Press

Loach K. (2023) *Oh Jeremy Corbyn: The Big Lie* [Film] London: Platform Films.

Marx K. (1988) *The Economic and Philosophic Manuscripts of 1844 and the Communist Manifesto (Great Books in Philosophy)* New York: Prometheus Books.

McCluskey L. (2021) *Always Red* New York: OR Books.

Parker L. (2016) *Apologies* [Film], London: Jerwood Arts.

Parker L. (2019) *Solidarity* [Film], London: City Projects.

Smith D. & Chamberlain P. (2016) *Blacklisted: The Secret War Between Big*

Business and Union Activists 2nd Edition, Oxford: New Internationalist.

Stanworth M. (1983) *Gender and Schooling: Study of Sexual Divisions in the Classroom (Explorations in Feminism)* London: Hutchinson.

Taylor L. (2016) *Thinking Allowed: Blacklisting* [radio] London: BBC Radio 4. Available at: https://www.bbc.co.uk/programmes/b07zzrkw

Tomlinson R. (2004) *Ricky* London: Sphere.

Tressell R. (1965) *The Ragged Trousered Philanthropists* St Albans: Panther.

Tribune (2022) 'The Pentonville 5 at 50', *Tribune,* 21 July, 2022. Available at: https://tribunemag.co.uk/2022/07/pentonville-five-1972-dockers-strike-industrial-relations-act

Wood L. (1979) *A Union to Build: The Story of UCATT* London: Lawrence & Wishart.

Printed in Great Britain
by Amazon